INDEX FUND INVESTING

A Comprehensive Beginner's Guide to Learn the Realms of Index Funding Investing A-Z and Grow your Income

➢ VON CLYDE ➣

©Copyright 2020 by Von Clyde- All rights reserved.

This document is geared towards providing exact and reliable information in regards to the topic and issue covered. The publication is sold with the idea that the publisher is not required to render accounting, officially permitted, or otherwise, qualified services. If advice is necessary, legal or professional, a practiced individual in the profession should be ordered.

From a Declaration of Principles which was accepted and approved equally by a Committee of the American Bar Association and a Committee of Publishers and Associations.

In no way is it legal to reproduce, duplicate, or transmit any part of this document in either electronic means or in printed format. Recording of this publication is strictly prohibited and any storage of this document is not allowed unless with written permission from the publisher. All rights reserved.

The information provided herein is stated to be truthful and consistent, in that any liability, in terms of inattention or otherwise, by any usage or abuse of any policies, processes, or directions contained within is the solitary and utter responsibility of the recipient reader. Under no circumstances will any legal responsibility or blame be held against the publisher for any reparation, damages, or monetary loss due to the information herein, either directly or indirectly.

Respective authors own all copyrights not held by the publisher.

The information herein is offered for informational purposes solely, and is universal as so. The presentation of the information is without contract or any type of guarantee assurance.

The trademarks that are used are without any consent, and the publication of the trademark is without permission or backing by the trademark owner. All trademarks and brands within this book are for clarifying purposes only and are the owned by the owners themselves, not affiliated with this document

Table of Contents

Introduction 1

Chapter 1: What is an Index Fund? 3
  Meaning of an Index 3
  What is an Index Fund? 4
  How Does an Index Fund Work? 6
  Classifications of Index Funds 8

Chapter 2: Steps of Buying an Index Fund 10

Chapter 3: Factors to Consider when Buying an Index Fund 15

Chapter 4: Top Five Stock Market Indices You Need to Know 18
  S&P 500 (Standard and Poors) 18
  Dow Jones Industrial Average (DJIA) 20
  NASDAQ 21
  Russel 2000 23
  CRSP US Total Market Index 24
  Criteria for Selecting the Right Stock Market Index 24

Chapter 5: Top Five Index Funds to Invest in 2019-2020 26
  Vanguard S&P 500 ETF 26
  Fidelity Zero Large Cap Index 28

SPDR S&P 500 ETF Trust 29
iShares Core S&P 500 EFT 30
Schwab S&P 500 Index 30

Chapter 6: Passive Investment 33
Types of Passive Investments 33
Benefits of Passive Investment 37
Features of Passive Investing 39
The Role of Passive Managers 40
Benefits of Passive Investing 41
Risks of Passive Investing 42

Chapter 7: Investing in an Index Fund 43
Investing in an Index Fund 43
Why you Need to Invest in an Index Fund 44
Bond Index Fund 49
Bond Mutual Funds and ETFs Performance 51
Stock Index Fund 51

Chapter 8: Fundamentals of Investments 55
Investment Goals/Reasons 55
Tracking Errors 56

Chapter 9: Investment Principles 57

Chapter 10: Exchange-Traded Funds (ETFs) 61
What is an ETF? 61
History of ETFs 61
How do ETFs Operate? 62

The Creation of ETFs 62
Redemption of ETFs 63
Trading in ETFs 63
Pricing of ETFs 65
Benefits of ETFs 65
Top Five Reasons Why You Need to Invest in ETFs 66
Important Factors You Need to Consider Before Investing in ETFs 67

Chapter 11: Open Ended Investment Companies (OEICs) 71
What are OEICs? 71
How Do OEICs Work? 71
Structure of an OEIC 72
The Benefits of Open-Ended Funds 73
Pricing of an OEIC 74
Where Can you Buy/Sell OEICs Products? 74
What is the Difference between OEIC and Unit Trusts? 75
Charges and Costs 75
Income Distributions/Returns 76
Risks Involved in OEICs 77
Diversification of OEICs 77
Investment Styles Used in OEICs 78

Chapter 12: Unit Trusts 80
Meaning of a Unit Trust 80
How Does a Unit Trust Work? 80
What Are the Investment Styles for a Unit Trust? 81

Different Types of Funds Under a Unit Trust 82

Benefits of a Unit Trust.. 83

Pricing of a Unit Trust 84

Costs Associated with Unit Trusts 85

Returns: Capitals Gains and Dividends Payouts 85

When is the best time to invest in unit trusts? 86

Active and Index Investing Styles 86

The Procedures of Redeeming Funds from a Unit of Trust...... 87

Type of Taxes you are Required to Pay 88

Monitoring Daily Prices 89

Switching of Funds.. 89

Chapter 13: Investment Trust 90

What is an Investment Trust? 90

Key Features of Investment Trusts.. 94

The Unpopularity of Investment Trusts 97

Sectors of Investment Trust 99

Types of Investment Trusts 100

Benefits of an Investment Trust 101

Investment Trusts and Real Assets.. 101

Investment Trusts and Private Equity 102

Costs Involved when Buying or Selling an Investment Trust . 104

Chapter 14: Mutual Funds 106

What are Mutual Funds?.. 106

Features of Mutual Funds 108

Charges of Mutual Fund Scheme 111

Benefits of Mutual Funds Investment 113
Asset Allocation in Mutual Funds 114
Things to Consider Before Investing in Mutual Funds 114
Types of Mutual Fund Schemes 116
Costs Associated with Mutual Funds Investing 118
Returns from Mutual Funds Investment 118

Chapter 15: The Role of Diversification in Investment 120
What is Diversification? 120
What Determines the Asset Class in Your Portfolio? 121
The History of Diversification 122
About Systematic and Unsystematic Risks 123
National and International Diversification 124
Optimal Number of Securities in a Portfolio 126
Factors Influencing Your Portfolio Size 126
How to Build a Well Diversified Portfolio 127

Chapter 16: Portfolio Risk Management 129
What is Risk Management? 129
Measurement of Risk 130
Risk Tolerance 133

Chapter 17: Portfolio Management 136
Meaning of Portfolio Management 136
The Role of Portfolio Management 137
The Process of Portfolio Management 137
The Key Elements of Portfolio Management 139
Portfolio Management in Passive Investment 141

Portfolio Management in Active Investment 142

Benefits of Portfolio Management 143

Conclusion 145

References 148

Introduction

If you are an investor or a scholar, be assured that you are in the right place and at the right time. Therefore, keep reading to get more information about the content of this resource.

As you peruse through this piece, it is vital to note that index funds have become the preferred investment vehicle to many institutional and retail investors around the world. The latest research indicates that retail investors were the majority (89%) who held the most significant part of $17.7 trillion in US mutual funds net assets as of 2018 (ICI, 2019).

Why are many retail investors interested in investing in index funds? What is so special about this mode of investment? By using this book, you will answer these questions and also get a relevant perspective regarding index funds.

In this book, you will learn more about index funds, and you will also get to know the reasons why you need to invest in them.

Through this book, you will find the crucial steps that you are supposed to take before injecting your hard-earned money into this particular investment. These steps are vital because they will guide you to make an informed choice and avoid latter regrets because of losses or risks.

Index funds are the most lucrative mode of investment in the world today. As an investor, you need proper guidance on the essential things to consider when buying an index fund. You need to know the technical aspects regarding this business model and relate them to the business world.

More importantly, by studying this text, you will understand how an index fund works and why it is more beneficial than other investments.

Through this book, you will get adequate information on why diversification is vital when it comes to investment. Index funds encompass a diversified portfolio. Comprehensive information is provided in the book regarding how the strategy of diversification helps to cushion your investment against losses.

In this book, you will get sufficient information on how you can diversify your investment portfolio, how you can manage risks, and how you can determine the optimal number of securities in a portfolio. Also, through this book, a lot has been revealed to you regarding various structures that offer index fund investing services. Therefore, as an investor, you have many alternatives where you can get your investment services. Enjoy your reading!

Chapter 1

What is an Index Fund?

Meaning of an Index

Before we delve into an index fund, it is vital to understand what an index is. An index is a list of stocks selected based on some rules. For instance, Standard and Poor's 500 comprises of a list of the best 500 stocks traded on the New York Stock Exchange.

What is a stock market index? It entails a weighted average of stocks that have been chosen to represent the overall market or a particular segment. Therefore, the performance of personal funds or stocks can be assessed against this index. Through the index, you can make informed decisions regarding market allocations of securities.

In the US, the New York Stock exchange started using the index in 1792. This was meant to assess the quality of the stock exchange. Therefore, that is when the stock market index came into being.

What are the common indices in the world today? The following is a brief description of renowned indices.

- **Dow Jones Industrial Average (DJIA):** This is a collection of 30 blue-chip stocks, and is a famous index of all time. It deals with large companies in the US

- **Nasdaq**: This index deals with companies in the technology sector, and it has all stocks related to this sector

- Russel 2000: It deals with small and medium companies and has 2000 shares.

- CRSP US Total Market Index: It covers the total market and has 4000 stocks.

- S&P500: S & P (Standard and Poor's 500) comprises a list of the best 500 stocks traded on the New York Stock Exchange.

It is vital to note that the indices are reviewed regularly to include or exclude stocks based on whether they are within the indices' metrics.

What is an Index Fund?

An index fund is a mutual fund that outsources the selection of securities to the experts or committees setting index methodologies. It is a collection of a portfolio (stocks and bonds) meant to match the accomplishment of a market index. Therefore, although an index fund has a portfolio manager, they don't make the selection of stocks or any other security for investors. The portfolio manager ensures that the fund gets results that are close to the index.

When did index funds come into being? Jack Boggle was the pioneer of the index fund. He invented this business model in 1975 to help retail investors compete with high-performing individuals and institutions.

Warren Buffet, though a proponent of active management, once expressed his support for passive investments. According to Dolvin (2015), Buffet opined that hedge funds and private equities made billions of money that benefitted the fund managers but not the clients. Therefore, investors are likely to get good returns if they invest in passive index funds.

The primary role of an index fund is to mimic the performance of a particular stock market index. Therefore, the index fund entails a collection of stocks that are similar to the index it is trying to mirror.

Due to the application of mimicking principle, index funds don't require a high rate of stock turnover to maintain performance like that of the index. The goal of an index fund is to offer an avenue whereby a diversified portfolio is bought using the economies of scale and at a low cost.

And what is a mutual fund? It is a collection of various types of investments, such as bonds and stocks. It is one of the most common and passive investments. In the US, passive investment methods such as mutual funds account for at least 45% of equity assets. A quite number of investors believe that mutual funds have good track records and low transaction costs.

You can participate in the investment of securities in two ways – passive and active management. Under active management, the investor does market research and purchases the securities on their own, whereas the passive approach entails investing in a portfolio of stock via an index fund.

What is the difference between an index fund and actively managed funds? For an actively managed fund, there's a paid manager whose role is to pick the best investments for the mutual fund. On the contrary, the index fund doesn't choose investments. Its primary purpose is to mimic the index it is trying to track in the market.

What are these committees setting up the index methodologies? The commonly known committees are The Wall Street Journal and the Standard & Poor 500. For instance, if you purchase a Dow Jones Industrial Average, the selection of securities under this index is made at the Wall Street Journal.

How Does an Index Fund Work?

Index funds work like active mutual funds. What they do is that they take investors' deposits and issue them with shares. Next, they use this money to buy shares of stock in the indexed firms or to pay investors who may wish to redeem their shares.

It is vital to note that an index fund operates by tracking an index? What do I mean? The fund is automated to detect a shift in values of the securities under a particular index. For instance, in the US, the S&P 500 index consists of 500 companies whose securities are traded on the New York Stock Exchange. If an index fund wants to track S&P 500, it would invest in all the 500 companies under the index.

The fund's responsibility to monitor the changes in stock prices to buy those securities joining the index and sell those leaving the index. This is the best strategy of ensuring that the fund's return mirrors that of a particular index.

Also, note that an index fund operates by matching the market's performance over time. The study shows that the market return's average annual performance is 9-10%. Therefore, by investing in an index fund, you are assured of getting excellent results at the end of a particular period.

An index fund also works like that of a mutual fund. However, under the mutual fund, the fund manager oversees the positions in the fund, meaning that they are the ones who buy and sell stocks. Also, note that in the actively managed mutual funds, huge expenses are incurred, and there is little benefit to the fund managers and the investors.

As for index funds, the decision to manage positions is outsourced to the professionals responsible for creating the index. Therefore, fund managers aren't paid to make positions.

The primary responsibility of an Index fund's portfolio manager is to get results that are near the index. They do this by purchasing and disposing of assets when they join or leave the index list.

It is essential to note that an index fund doesn't perform exactly as the index under track because it is affected by operating and transaction costs.

Index funds, such as ETF (Exchange Traded Fund), are transacted daily like stock. Therefore, their prices are determined by the forces of demand and supply. Traditionally, an investor paid a commission when transacting in ETFs. However, due to competition, a quite number of brokers are charging very little or no commission when you are buying or selling ETFs.

Classifications of Index Funds

How are index funds classified? As you select an index fund, note that they are categorized based on the following aspects – the type of assets, technology, finance, consumer staples, transport, geographical orientation, and company size and market capitalization. It is vital to get the perspective of this classification so that you may make the right selection. The following is a brief highlight of these categorizations.

- Types of assets: These are funds which operate by tracking bonds (both domestic and foreign), commodities, and cash.
- Technology: This is index deals with companies offering technological services such as Google and Facebook
- Finance: This index constitutes companies providing financial services such as Citigroup
- Consumer goods: This index involves consumer staples organizations such as Coca Cola.

- Transports: This index entails companies in the transport sector, such as American Airlines and Delta.

- Geographical orientation: These funds handle stocks that are transacted on foreign exchanges. For instance, the Vanguard emerging markets stock index fund provides investors with exposure to the upcoming markets.

- The size of the company and its market capitalization: Index funds are classified based on the sizes of the companies they track. For example, some funds deal with small and medium enterprises, while others handle large companies.

It is crucial to find out the classification of the index fund you want to invest with to have a clear perspective of the various stocks under its list. This will enable you to make an informed opinion on where to invest your hard-earned money.

Chapter 2

Steps of Buying an Index Fund

In case you have made a decision to invest in index funds, it is vital to go through the following steps to comprehend what it entails to purchase these products.

Step One: Find out where to buy

There are two common options where you can buy your index fund – Mutual Fund Company or brokerage firm. You can also buy it from exchange-traded funds (ETFs). ETFs are small mutual funds which are transacted like socks on a daily basis.

The following tips will help make a brilliant choice on where to buy the index funds.

Select a Convenient Company

For the easy of a transaction, find a provider who can accord you all types of services under one roof. For instance, a discount broker might be the best choice for you because they deal with both index funds and stocks.

Transaction Costs

Find out the amount the broker or the fund company charges when trading in an index fund. If you want to evaluate the fund, consider its net returns. Ensure that the fund companies you are analyzing quote net returns of all costs. When choosing the best index fund, assess them based on their expenses and net returns

Withstanding difficult circumstances

As you evaluate the funds, consider those who have been withstanding difficult times, such as recession and bull and bear markets.

The reputation of the fund manager and the firm

Investigate the fund and its management through its registration agency, such as the security and exchange commission. Check press releases to see whether there is anything negative about the company and its administrators. You can also do a search in Google to find out if there is any negative review against the firm. If there isn't, then shortlist the company and proceed to the next step.

Explore Commission Free Options

When investing, any money saved can count a lot for you. Are there transaction-free ETFs? If you find them, give them consideration.

Funds Selection

If you want to purchase a variety of index funds from different companies, then you can quickly get this service from a discount broker.

Step Two: Select an index

Before putting your money in the investment, do your research and decide where exactly you want to venture in. For instance, select an index based on whether it is dealing with the products you are interested in. If you are going to invest in stocks related to technology, then go for the index that handles it.

There are thousands of ETFs, and, therefore, you need to take your time to select the one that is cheaper in costs but with maximum returns.

Many index funds operate based on the stocks or assets they are involved in. For example, the S&P 500 is one of the best indexes because of its track record with 500 renowned companies in the US. These companies are significant in the US economy, and they represent various industries.

Step Three: Decide how you will purchase the funds

Depending on what you want and your convenience, you can buy the funds either from a mutual fund or a broker. Brokers are the best option if you want to enquire and purchase many products under one roof. Also, find out the mode of payment required by different companies and decide the one to use.

Step Four: Find out the investment costs

Most of the index funds are characterized by low costs but do your research to select the cheapest because not all of them are cheap. For example, ETFs are affordable and can give you diversification while investing with them. In case you are inexperienced in matters of investment analysis, consult a financial advisor.

Why is it less costly to manage an index fund? The buying and selling of positions are outsourced to experts who run the indexes. They are also cheap to manage since they are automated to trace the changes in value in an index.

Although index funds are not run by a huge team of professionals, they do incur administration costs. These costs are deducted from the individual shareholder's investment. However, index funds have been proven to be the best mode of investment because they yield more returns than other instruments under active management.

A group of funds may have similar goals, e.g., tracking of S&P 500, but their management costs are different. Consider the fund with the lowest proportion of administrative expenses. The difference in proportions regarding the management costs may seem small to you, but what matters a lot is the returns you will accrue from your long term investment. Also, bear in mind that bigger funds are associated with small fees.

The following is a highlight of what to consider when assessing the costs of investment

Check the minimum fund required to invest in an index fund

Depending on your budget, consider the minimum amount of investment required by different funds to make an informed decision on where to invest. For instance, mutual funds have a high minimum investment in contrast to ETFs which can be purchased via the share. Please note that after you have bought your investment, the funds will allow you to add more money later on.

Check the account minimum

The account minimum is not the same as the investment minimum. It means the minimum value of the fund that shall remain in your account without being redeemed. Most funds have an account minimum of zero. As an investor, consider companies with no account minimum.

Consider the tax-cost ratio

Investing in an index fund can attract capital gain taxes. Before making any investment, research companies that are enjoying tax benefits. For instance, you may consider tax-efficient ETFs that are operating in a taxable account such as an IRA.

Step Five: Choose the right asset mix

Choosing the right asset mix is vital for your excellent returns and risk minimization. When making the allocations, ensure that the ratio of a bond to stocks is favorable to your financial situation and is geared towards your retirement age. The right asset mix is essential because it influences the return and risk of your portfolio.

Step Six: Monitoring your portfolio

This requires periodic checking to see how your investment is fairing. If, for instance, you realize that your allocation is of the target by 10%, then you should rebalance your assets. Rebalancing means selling a stock that is not doing well and buying a different one, which you think is performing better. You can also change your asset mix by injecting extra funds, probably on an annual basis.

Chapter 3

Factors to Consider when Buying an Index Fund

Index funds are among the best business models that can earn you good returns within a particular time. Before you invest in them, read through the following factors that are essential in shaping your wise investment decisions.

- The efficiency of the index fund: You can determine if an index fund is run efficiently by checking whether it's mirroring the performance of the underlying index. To gather this information, view the index fund's returns on its quote page. This page gives you crucial information regarding the fund's returns versus the benchmark index over a particular period.

Are the returns identical? Don't worry if you note some disparities. The small difference could be because of administration costs and taxes. However, avoid funds whose performances lag the index by more than the expense ratio.

- The cost of the index fund: It is better to invest in an index fund, such ETF, than in a mutual fund. An exchange-traded fund (ETF) is cheaper, and it gives you an option of buying just a portion of the fund. It is essential to bear in mind that ETFs and mutual funds pool investors' money into a variety of securities, and help them to diversify, purchase, and manage their assets.

According to Phoon and Koh (2017), ETFs, a type of index fund, are the favorite of many people currently. They are inexpensive and guarantees excellent returns to individual investors. For instance, their expense ratio could be a minimum of 0.03%, implying that for every $ 1, 000 investment, investors incur an expense of $0.3 per year.

- Investment returns: The main reason why you invest is because of expecting good returns. The most significant proportion of the performance is determined by market forces, something you can't control. Therefore, if you invest in an index fund for an extended period, you are likely to get excellent results.

- Investment Risk: Investment is associated with some levels of risks that you need to manage. Risk means that you are uncertain of the return you will get from your investment. If you are after high returns, then you should accept the uncertainty that you will get them.

- Asset allocation: It entails dividing your money among different types of investments. You can invest in any of the investment categories – cash, bonds, stocks, etc. Note that appropriate asset allocation is vital because it enhances diversification. Before investing, chose an index which deals with the products you are interested in.

Before you invest in an index fund, you need to familiarize yourself with passive investment. This is because an index fund is one of the structures which offer passive investment services. The following (chapter four) gives a detailed description of passive investment.

If you want to make prudent decisions in your investment, you need to understand how various indexes operate. The following chapter gives an overview of the top five stock market indices in the world.

Chapter 4

Top Five Stock Market Indices You Need to Know

Are you familiar with the leading stock market indices in the world? This section will elaborate below on the different leading stock market indices that you need to know.

S&P 500 (Standard and Poors)

It's an index in the US that has the responsibility of monitoring the stocks of approximately 500 influential companies. It also provides monitoring on the stock's performance and can detect and report any risks that may occur. Most of the investors use this index to measure the health status of the US economy.

When was S&P 500 index founded? The stock market index was founded in 1957 by Standard and Poor's so that it can give track of the value of 500 large companies that were on the exchange (NYSE) list. The S&P 500 has been performing well as compared to bonds since the date of inception. The latest market capitalization of the subject index is US$25,951,050.9 million as of September 30^{th,} 2019 (Siblisresearch, 2019).

Having an idea as an investor of how a stock market index is weighted is very crucial. How are the components of the index weighted? The free-float methodology is used to weigh the components. This method involves computing the equity price and performing multiplication of it with the number of shares that are available in the market. Larger companies such as Apple impact the value of the S&P 500 more as compared to the smaller companies. From 1979 to 2019, Microsoft Corporation has the largest weighting, with a rate of 3.83%. Apple Incorporation comes second with a rate of 3.60%, and Amazon comes third on the list with a rate of 3.11%.

What makes the S&P 500 stock market index much popular in the US?

- It is much popular because of its wide coverage since it tracks the stock's performance of the largest companies in the US. The S&P 500 stock market index is, therefore, able to provide a broader view of the economic status of the United States.

- The S&P 500 index makes an update on its components quarterly as compared to other indices. It makes it accurate when studying the market capitalization of the state.

What are the downsides of employing the index?
- It does not consider assets such as cash and bonds possessed by an investor. It mostly focuses on the stock of the investor, excluding other assets.

- S&P index is only efficient for large companies with a large market capitalization as compared to small companies. Small companies or individual investors who use the index as their indicator result with an inaccurate measure of the stock's performance.

- The great impact on the index is mostly contributed by the largest 50 companies in the US that cover almost half the value of the index.

Dow Jones Industrial Average (DJIA)

It keeps track of 30 powerful public companies that perform their exchange on both the NYSE and NASDAQ. DJIA got its name in 1896 from its founders named Charles Dow together with his business partner, Edward Jones. It first began as an index for only 12 companies in the US whose sectors were tobacco and cotton. It later expanded to 30 stocks in 1928. Investors refer to this index as a bundle of companies with stable earnings since it comprises of Walt Disney Company and the Exxon Mobil Corporation.

The latest market capitalization of the Dow Jones Industrial Average index is US$7916.17 billion as of 29th November 2019. Apple incorporation was the leading company in the market capitalization of the index with US$1152.72 billion as of 7th November 2019. Moreover, Microsoft Corporation came the second leading company with US$1100.53 billion as of 7th November 2019.

DJIA stock market index components are weighted using the price-weighted methodology, unlike the index mentioned above. How does the price-weighted method work? Companies associated with this index have their rankings depending on their share prices. A company with a greater share price will have more weight as compared to a company with a lower share price. A stock worth US$200 will have more weighting than a $100 stock. Any changes that take place in the 30 stocks will make the index have the same effect in the number of points. As of 27th November 2019, Boeing Company had the highest weight, followed by the UnitedHealth Group Incorporated, and then Apple Incorporation came third.

What makes the DJIA index popular in the US? Dow Jones Industrial Average index tells a broader view of the economy in the US. It's because the companies that are associated with this index include all industries other than transportation.

The downside of the index is that many individuals think DJIA is not a good indicator of the US economy due to the fragmentation and dispersion of the stock market. Technology changes, and the advancement of the worldwide web contribute to it.

NASDAQ

NASDAQ is a stock market index of around 3300 securities. The 300 securities comprise indexes such as common stock and investment trusts for real estate. It excludes ETFs, debentures, and preferred shares. NASDAQ was founded on 4th February 1971 by Gordon Macklin with an initial value of 100. The latest market capitalization of the NASDAQ index is $US17.26 billion as of 29th

November 2019. The computation of the market capitalization of the index is by multiplying the price of the stock with the outstanding shares of the company. (macrotrends)

How is the NASDAQ index weighted? The index is weighted using the market capitalization method. Companies are assigned weights based on market capitalization. The bigger the company, the higher the shared weight, and therefore it will have a greater impact on the index. The total amount then goes through some adjustments using the divisor mechanism to enable appropriate figures for reporting purposes.

NASDAQ index concentrates on the technology industries that, as of May 9th, 2018, had weights of 46. 40%, services by consumers had 20.16%, and care from the health sector had 10.86%. Apple Incorporation was the leading company with the highest weight (12.078) as of 27th November 2019. Microsoft Corporation came second on the leading board with a weight of 11.605 and then followed by Amazon Incorporation with a weight of 8.978.

Why is NASDAQ popular?

- NASDAQ is efficient even for small companies to use as compared to other indices.
- The index listing fees are lower and affordable for small companies.

The downside of the NASDAQ index is that it does not have specialists who handle the exchange platform and therefore becomes problematic.

Russel 2000

How well do you know the Russel 2000 index? It's an index that offers monitoring and performance evaluation of around 2000 small companies in the Russel 3000 stock market index. It comprises a two-third segment of the Russel 3000 index that is a larger stock market index in the US. Frank Ressel Company founded the Russel 2000 index in 1984. The index is mostly used to measure the performance of small-capitalization stocks in the US economy. The latest average market capitalization of the Russel 2000 index was $2.25 billion as of September 2019.

Having an idea of the weighting method of the index is very crucial and will help you in formulating your investing strategy. The weighting method for the Russel 2000 stock market index is the float market capitalization methodology. It does not include companies with market capitalization lower than $30 million and also the trading stocks below $1.00 per share. The components of the Russel 2000 index are evaluated using a formula, unlike the S&P 500 index that determines its components by a committee.

What makes Russel 2000 stock market index popular?

- It tracks the performance of the stock of companies with small capitalization.
- It uses a formula to determine its components, unlike other indices that employ a committee.

Its downside is that investors with much reliance on the index may not diversify across other sectors in the economy.

CRSP US Total Market Index

It's an index associating with 4000 equities of the US. It first appeared on the NASDAQ feed on January 18th, 2011. The index includes the market securities in the NYSE. Its return gain for the first year was 15.43% as of 29th November 2019. The latest market capitalization was $2311.10 as of 29th November 2019.

The index comprises of Real Estate Investment Trust and common stock. The components of the stock market index are weighted and using the float market capitalization methodology. It normally happens quarterly. The CRPS US Total Market Index includes a stock when it complies with the below requirements:

- The company must exceed a market capitalization of $15 million.
- The float shares of the company must exceed 12.5% of the total shares.

Criteria for Selecting the Right Stock Market Index

- Check on the size of the index. Different stock market indices have varying sizes. You should choose the index with the right size that will well suit your company. Large stock market indices are more powerful than the smaller indices.
- Size of the company. An index that associates with small capitalized company tend to have more returns but with large market volatility as compared to the index that is

associated with large capitalized companies that have smaller market volatility.

I trust that you are now knowledgeable on matters regarding the best stock market indices in the world. Next, you also need insights into the top five index funds in the world. The next chapter will guide you on this.

Chapter 5

Top Five Index Funds to Invest in 2019-2020

Index funds can be mutual funds or even exchange-traded funds that monitor and give tracking of the stock market index. They assure the investors on ownership of stocks at a lower price and risks. Below are the leading index funds you can invest in 2019.

Vanguard S&P 500 ETF

It's an index fund that gives track and provides investment on stocks belonging to the Standard &Poor's 500. It's a powerful fund in the US since it possesses assets worth $119 billion as of July 2019. Vanguard S&P 500 exchange-traded fund started in 2010, founded by John Bogle, and it is under the support of Vanguard.

Let us now narrow down into the Vanguard ETF and mutual funds. Vanguard ETFs have lower expense ratios and therefore provide investment opportunities for companies with large and even small capitalization. There exist around 17 Vanguard ETF products that are more focused on the stocks in the US. Vanguard assigns different ETFs as growth ETF, value ETF, or even the blend ETF.

Growth ETF provides investment for stocks that are above the average level.

Conversely, value ETF offers investment for stocks that are below the average level. Blend Vanguard ETF does a combination of the two ETFs. You can start Vanguard mutual funds with a minimum investment of $3000. It shares price once every day, unlike the Vanguard ETFs that can be purchased and offered for sale throughout the day. Many investors prefer the Vanguard ETFs to mutual funds because of their lower expense ratios. You can purchase and sell the Vanguard products through a Vanguard brokerage account.

What are your investing goals?

Do you know you can make your college dreams a reality by using a Vanguard account? You can achieve this by having your savings on the Vanguard account. Below are the steps you need to follow to start up with your college savings:

- Look for the appropriate account for the savings.
- Select the right investments for your account.
- Register the account online to start with the savings.

You cannot lose the college savings even if you don't make it to college. The funds can be used to pay for other vocational fees, or a family member can use the funds for his or her college. You can use the 529 saving plan that will help you in selecting the right account for your college savings. 529 saving plan assists your account to grow and becomes closer to your education goals. It also assists you not to pay the federal taxes on the earnings of the college account. You pay for your taxes when you make a withdrawal of the money in the account.

What are the benefits of using the Vanguard S&P 500 ETF?

- You pay for no commission when you purchase or offer the index fund for sale using your Vanguard account.

- You can invest in Vanguard mutual funds with as little as $1000 for retirement funds. Most of the funds normally require a minimum investment of $3000.

- Vanguard S&P 500 ETF has great returns on the first, third and fifth period of years with respective gains of 9.40%, 13.46%, and 10.86%

Fidelity Zero Large Cap Index

It is the index fund used for investment for almost all stocks in the US except for companies with a market capitalization of less than $25 million. It uses the share symbol of FNILX. Fidelity Zero Large Cap Index has around 2500 holdings because of performing investment with larger companies in the US that build its portfolio.

It includes companies that are on Fidelity U.S Large Capthat is a weighted index for market capitalization, which evaluates the performance of stocks of large capitalized companies. The leading holding of the index is the Microsoft Corporation with 4.21%, and Apple Incorporation comes second with 3.95% as of 29th November 2019.

The index is quite similar to the S&P 500 index fund. Fidelity Zero Large Cap Index has great returns on the first, third, and sixth monthly periods with respective gains of 3.66%, 7.92%, and 14.17% as of November 29^{th,} 2019 (Siblisresearch, 2019). FNILX has no expense ratio, unlike other index funds. The benefit of using the FNILX is that the fund is free.

SPDR S&P 500 ETF Trust

It's an acronym for the Standard & Poor's Depositary Receipt, and its symbol is SPY. The index gives track and monitors the Standard and Poor's 500performance. Its expense ratio is 0.0945%. SPDR Services LLC sponsors this index fund. The inception date of the fund was on 22nd January 1993 by the State Street Global Advisors. It then underwent design and development by the executives of the American Stock Exchange. It now appears on the NYSE list. The exchange takes place on the NYSE Arca. The fund was the first-ever ETF in the US.

The dividend distribution is quarterly, depending on the number of dividends the Trust has. The index fund has around 505 holdings as of 27th November 2019. It has great returns of the periods of one year with a rate of 14.16%, three-year with a rate of 14.75%, and five-year with a rate of 10.64% as of 31st October 2019. The fund has a weighted average market capitalization of $277,685.84 million as of 27th November 2019.

The fund is simple, with enough flexibility for trading. An investor can employ limit orders or even stop-loss orders, just like in stock trading. You can purchase or sell the fund through a brokerage account.

iShares Core S&P 500 EFT

It's an index fund in the USA with an expense ratio of 0.04% that monitors and gives tracks of the large indices. It's under the management of the iShares and has around 510 holdings. The leading holdings of the index fund are Microsoft Corporation, Apple, and Amazon Incorporations. It has great returns of the periods of one year with a rate of 16.22%, three-year with a rate of 14.87%, and five-year with a rate of 10.92% as of 29th November 2019.

The main sectors involved in the index fund are Technology (19.37%) and Financial (16.11%) services as of 27th November 2019. IVV has tiny charges as compared to the SPY index mentioned above. You can buy the iShares Core S&P 500 EFT index fund through the online brokerage accounts.

Due to its low cost, many investors prefer this index fund. The downside of employing the iShares Core S&P 500 EFT index fund is that it can result in a huge loss of money during periods of stock market recession.

Schwab S&P 500 Index

It's an index fund in the USA that also tracks and monitors the benchmark index, Standard &Poor's 500. It uses the symbol of SWPPX, and it is under the current management of FerianJuwono,

Christopher Bliss, and also SabyaSinha. It has 509 holdings of the largest companies in the US, with a low expense ratio (0.03%). The inception date of the index fund was on 19th May1997, and it's under the management of Schwab. The annual returns for the third and fifth-year are 12.3% and 8.4%, respectively, as of 29th November 2019.

The main costs involved in the index are publishing expenses and the expenses for the total net that have the rates of 0.09% and 0.0893% as of 26th November 2019. Other minor expenses include costs for registration, accounting services, auditing, advisor, and foreign tax expenses. The risks involved in the SWPPX are similar to those in the S&P 500 index.

What criteria should you implement when selecting the right index fund?

- Returns of the index fund. An index fund will have the same performance just as its benchmark index. Index funds with small capitalization can perform better in the long run than the funds with large market capitalization.

- You need to perform thorough research on the index fund before employing it on the market to shun from losses.

- Type of investment. It is upon you to decide on the type of investment you are going to handle. When you decide on long-term growth, you will need to employ stocks on your market. Conversely, an investor who decides on stability will need to employ bonds on the market.

I believe that you have now gotten sufficient information concerning the top five index funds in the world. It is vital to note that index fund investing is a business model that utilizes a passive investment approach.

What is a passive investment? The next chapter gives a comprehensive perspective on it.

Chapter 6

Passive Investment

It refers to a business strategy of enhancing high returns through cost reduction – minimization transactions regarding buying and selling. The best example is index investing. For instance, investors could decide to buy an index fund, such as Dow Jones and Industrial Average, and hold it for an extended period. Research indicates that a quite number of mutual fund assets are indexed to S&P 500 than other indices (Belasco, Finke, Nanigian, 2012). Consequently, the demand for S&P 500's assets has made their values to appreciate a lot in the market. In short, bear in mind that the values of companies within the index are higher relative to those outside it.

Types of Passive Investments

There are two main types of passive investments – index funds and exchange-traded funds.

Index Fund

As you have already seen, an index fund is a mutual fund with a portfolio whose purpose is to match a particular benchmark index in the market, such as S&P 500. Index funds have been touted as the best in holding portfolios for retirees' accounts, such as IRAs and 401k. It is essential to note that the portfolio of the fund changes with variations in its benchmark index.

Upon coming into existence in the 1970s, index funds made excellent returns for the many investors, particularly the retail ones. Later on, further progress was made in the 1990s when Exchange Traded Funds (ETFs) were conceived. ETFs brought a lot of convenience by allowing investors to transact in index funds as stocks.

Exchange-Traded Funds (ETFs)

It is a form of an investment fund that is traded on the stock exchange. It comprises a portfolio of securities, such as stocks, and their shares trade daily like ordinary stocks. An example of EFT is SPDR S&P 500 EFT, which matches the S&P 500 index. The unique aspect of EFT is that they are marketable and can take any form, such stocks, bonds, commodities, and a mixture of investment types.

ETFs, a collection of securities, are traded on the stock exchange daily, whereas mutual funds are only transacted once a day when the market closes. Buying ETFs is economical to you because you are likely to enjoy low expense ratios and reduced brokerage charges than if you were to buy them individually. The value of an ETF share varies daily as different shares are transacted on the market.

An ETF is considered to be a diversified portfolio because it holds a mixture of assets. You can invest in ETFs for several reasons – to earn income, for speculation, hedging, etc. ETFs occur in different forms, as described below.

Bonds

These are fixed-income securities from government, companies, and local/state agencies. Trading on these instruments can be done electronically or over the counter.

One setback you need to know about bonds is that their liquidity is limited; however, we have some, which are exceptional. If you are an investor who wants to venture into bond business, then embrace ETF as a mean of achieving your goals.

In the past, trading on bonds was marred by opaque practices; their prices were only transparent to institutional investors. However, currently, things have changed – historical and current prices regarding bond ETF are known to ordinary investors.

By being illiquid, bonds are unlikely to be disposed of until maturity. This makes it difficult for an ETF to track a benchmark index in the market. It is vital to note that government bonds are more marketable than corporate bonds. This implies that for a state bond, you can easily dispose of it on a secondary market because of its high demand.

Then how do dealers of bond ETFs achieve their tracking? The liquidity issues surrounding these instruments have been an obstacle to match an ETF performance with market indices. Therefore, these funds track only representative samples for an index. For your information, please note that only the most liquid bonds are used as representatives.

The disadvantage of bond ETFs is that you have to pay for an annual management fee. But this shouldn't make you scary from investing; after all, if the fee charged is reasonable, go for the investment.

Sector Exchange Traded Funds

This one tracks indices dealing with different sectors, such as banking, oil & gas, and real estate. Therefore, a sector ETF does business by investing in the securities of a particular sector and then starts tracking companies under specific indices. It is essential to bear in mind that you can use a sector ETF to invest in all the securities belonging to a particular industry instead of dealing with single stocks.

With sector ETFs, there are minimal tracking errors because the underlying index's securities are highly tradable.

Commodity Exchange Traded Funds

They invest in various products, such as oil or consumer staples. Therefore, a commodity ETF invests in goods belonging to different sectors, e.g., agriculture and natural resources. The ETF can either hold the commodity physically or invest in it through futures contracts. The primary function of a commodity ETF is to track an underlying index which deals with different products.

To invest in a commodity, note that you rarely own a physical asset, but you sign some contracts backed by the product. The commonly traded commodities include precious metals, such as silver, bronze, gold, etc. A commodity ETF works by tracking the accomplishment of a particular product or group of commodities.

Currency Exchange Traded Funds

They make investments in foreign currencies such as Euro or USD. A currency EFT's primary goal is to expose your investment to forex currencies. Therefore, the ETF tracks the benchmark currency which is either based in one or many countries. This type of passive investments can help venture into forex businesses without participating in any act of trade. They can also be useful in speculating foreign currencies, diversification, or hedging.

Inverse Exchange Traded Funds: Their primary purpose is to achieve gains by shorting stocks; for instance, they sell a stock when they expect them to decline in value, expecting to repurchase them again at a lower price.

Note that you can transact in ETFs through online brokers or by visiting the offices of traditional dealers. Before you spend your money, do thorough research to compare costs and gains to maximize your investment value.

Benefits of Passive Investment

- It enhances diversification

Having a diversified is crucial for your investment's value maximization. Study shows that investing through index funds is the appropriate way of achieving diversification. Through index funding, there is a widespread of risks across the securities under a particular portfolio; for example, a loss in one stock is compensated by again from a different one.

- It is characterized by reduced fees and expenses

An index fund's primary function is to track an underlying index, but not to look for winners. By so doing, the sell or buying of securities is minimized; hence, achieving low operating expenses.

- Passive investment is under the management of experts

With index investing, you delegate the management function to experts and instead do other things that are helpful to you.

- It promotes transparent transactions

With index funds, you can tell the type of securities under a particular fund in a specific period. For instance, S&P 500 constitute the best 500 stocks traded on the New York Stock Exchange.

- The process of investment is simple

With the passive investment, you don't have to hassle doing research to determine the suitability of a particular index. Once you pay, the rest of the process is done by experts.

- It has a better tax efficiency than active investment:

Index funds entail the buying and holding of securities for an extended period. Therefore, there is minimal buying and selling of assets hence reduced capital gains taxes.

On the flip side, passive investment is highly exposed to market risks. For instance, when the prices of securities fall in the market, the index funds also decline. Also, fund managers are inflexible; they are prohibited from disposing of any security even if they expect its fall in price.

What is an active investment? It entails the selling and buying of securities in order to outperform a certain benchmark. With this approach, individual investors buy stocks, monitor their performance, and sell them later for a gain.

Active investors are not long-term oriented but are only interested in short-term financial gains. They operate by monitoring the market daily to detect price movements.

Features of Passive Investing

The following are the key features of passive investing

- Passive investing embraces a buy-and-hold technique for a certain period. Since there is reduced selling or buying of securities, the amount of capital gain tax is minimized. Through index funds, the investors seek to mimic the market index. The practice of mirroring the fund's performance with the benchmarks ensures that the former produces results that match the latter.

- The process of investment is very cheap, less sophisticated, and simple to understand. This means that there are no complicated procedures involved when you start executing your first investment.

- Passive investment produces excellent after-tax results overtime. Why? Since there is minimal selling and buying of securities, the amount of capital gains tax is reduced; hence, good annual results.

- Not influenced by price fluctuations: In index funds, the portfolio managers have no control over the sell and buying of stocks. Therefore, when there are price fluctuations, no transaction is executed on the securities belonging to the fund until when their time is due.

- The belief that long-term investment gives excellent profits: Passive investors embrace the idea of buying and holding for quite long in trust that they will get excellent gains at the end of the period.

The Role of Passive Managers

Passive managers play crucial roles regarding the matters of portfolio management. The following is a brief highlight of their roles.

- Matching market or sector performance: The primary function of a portfolio manager is to ensure that the performance of the fund is close to the underlying index they are mimicking. The fund managers achieve this through prudent cost management.

- Build a portfolio which matches the performance of a particular index in the market

- Doesn't do stock picking or market timing: With passive investment, portfolio managers have no control to sell or buy the securities based on price fluctuations.
- Rebalancing of securities to maintain their presence in the benchmark: Rebalancing entails realigning the composition of a portfolio of assets. The realignment is conducted periodically by selling or buying assets in a portfolio to maintain the original asset allocation.

Benefits of Passive Investing

Successful investment calls for the adoption and maintenance of a diversified portfolio. Therefore, index funding is one of the avenues you can use to attain appropriate diversification.

- They avoid frequent sell of securities, and they, therefore, incur lower transaction costs. They operate by tracking a target benchmark, and they minimize risks by holding all the securities in the indices they are dealing with.
- Simple to transact in an index fund, no complicated procedures. You don't have to engage with individual managers. Once you invest in an index fund, you just sit and wait. You don't have to carry out any research concerning the assets is before and after you invest.
- High transparency: There is openness on which securities are in a particular fund

- Tax-efficient model of doing business: reduced transactions under index fund ensures that capital gains tax are minimized

Risks of Passive Investing

The following are some of the risks encountered in passive investing. You need to beware of them so that you make a formed decision regarding your investment.

- Marketrisks: When the securities' market prices fall, the index funds also declines.

- Index fund managers aren't flexible. They have no power to sell securities even if prices are on a downward trend.

- Passive investments are confined to a particular index. Once you buy the securities under a certain fund, you have to stick there despite what is happening in the market.

- Small returns: Since their core business is to track a certain benchmark, they find it difficult to beat the market.

Passive investing can be an ideal option when you are not able to manage your investment. The best thing about it is that the management of your portfolio is done by experts.

Now you have gathered adequate information regarding an index, index fund, passive investments, and many more. The next chapter gives you a brief overview of investing in an index fund.

Chapter 7

Investing in an Index Fund

Investing in an Index Fund

Before investing in an index fund, you must carry out adequate research to get insights regarding the portfolio and the company you are about to deal with. Although index fund companies are the best you can invest with, you should determine the best asset allocation before making any investment. When you are ready to buy the funds, select a suitable one based on expense ratio and the index you want to track.

Also, make sure that you select an index fund with a minimum expense ratio. Why? A large expense ratio will lead to a reduction in your returns. After you have bought your first fund, you may continue investing on a monthly basis.

According to Boggle (2017), market timing, characterized by buying and selling of stocks, can make you lose your asset value. Boggle advises that if you want your money to grow in the market, you must keep it simple, and avoid acting based on your emotions.

What are Exchange Trade Funds (ETFs)? These are like mutual funds and are offered at expense ratios. However, there is a slight difference between the two. ETFs are transacted throughout the day, just like stocks, whereas mutual funds are traded at the end of the day.

Why you Need to Invest in an Index Fund

Index funds are the most rewarding investment products we have in the market today. The following is a brief description of the reasons why you need to invest in them.

> **Transfer of managerial responsibility to experts:** With an index fund, you don't have to manage the portfolio on your own. All the administration duties ale left in the hands of financial experts. After you make an investment, you wait to reap your returns at the end of a particular period
>
> **No need for researching too much about the instruments:** An index fund is a collection of a specific number of stocks representing a market. Experts have selected the stock on this list because they are the best in terms of performance. Therefore, you don't have to do investigations to establish the suitability of the stocks you want to buy.
>
> **Diversification:** An index fund is a collection of various stocks belonging to different companies. Investing in them is the best way of achieving diversification of your assets. This implies that if one stock in your portfolio loses, your value is compensated by a gain in another stock.

> **Tax efficiency:** unlike managed funds, there is minimal buying and selling in index funds. This means that capital gain tax is minimized.
>
> **A better way of avoiding psychological hurdles:** When you buy stocks as in individual, you are likely to sell them at one point because of impulse or market fear of loss. However, with index funds, your investment is held for a particular time under the management of financial experts. Therefore, you can't sell it on the basis of fear or ignorance.

As you all know, an index fund can either be an ETF or a mutual fund that provides storage for securities in a stock market index. Where can you purchase the index funds? You can get index funds from an online broker or an index fund provider. Vanguard is a common index provider in the US market. You need to be cautious when selecting the right online broker for your index funds. Different brokers have different charging fees.

Choosing the right broker will save you a lot of money. You need to employ the criteria below when choosing the right broker:

> The analog broker or the Robo-fund advisor. The traditional brokers give you the chance to make investing decisions. Its main benefit is that you incur lower costs since you have control over your investment. The downside of a traditional broker is that it needs attention since it's not automatic, unlike a Robo-fund advisor. Robo advisors are automated accounts that do all the investing work for you. They are

efficient and simple to utilize. Its main drawback is its high costs, unlike when employing traditional brokers.

Fees employed. The cost of market securities is a crucial factor for any trading. You need to select a broker who provides index funds with lower fees. It will help you save a lot of hundreds other than paying for high commission fees. The common fee charged by online brokers is around $10 per trade. You will be lucky enough if you come across a broker who charges no commission fees.

Diversity of the index funds. You need to select a broker who offers a wide variety of index funds. It will help you to try out different ETFs and mutual funds available in the market.

Platform's complexity. You need to select s broker who has index funds platforms that are ease of use. A platform that is easier to understand and operate with a simpler user interface. Do not purchase index funds from a broker with a complex platform that will make you confused.

Some common examples of the traditional brokers are Vanguard and Charles Schwab. Conversely, an example of the Robo-advisor is Betterment.

What are the things to put under consideration before investing in an index fund?

- Fund's expense ratio. It's a cost expressed as a percentage that comes up after deducting some costs on the return gained by the shareholder.

- The initial minimal requirement. It's the amount that you, as an investor, is supposed to know to accumulate enough funds.

- Minimal cost of the account. It is the account fee that you pay for when you purchase an account from a broker. Investors who purchase traditional accounts are likely to evade the account fees.

- Tax ratio. An index fund with a higher tax ratio contributes to higher capital gains taxes that may affect your investment returns.

An asset mix is a procedure of assigning different investments to different classes of assets. It's the mix-up of market stocks, bonds, and money securities in the market. The three classes comprise stocks for small, large, and medium capitalized companies, investment funds for real estate, and securities from a foreign country. An asset mix criteria assist you in reducing risks when investing in index funds as you desire to achieve your investment goals.

To select the right asset mix, you need to comply with the following

- **Set your objectives and your time horizon.**

It's the process that you ought to follow. You need to formulate objectives and be able to know how much time you are to spend to achieve your objectives. It also points out the risks that may occur in the process of achieving your objectives.

The longer the period you have, the more risks you can take on the market using different classes of the assets.

- **Know your risk tolerance.**

It's all about knowing the risk level you want on your investments. You identify your risk tolerance when creating an investment account. A Robo-advisor will impose a questionnaire that helps in determining risk tolerance. It assists in the whole investment process. Investors who are riskier tend to invest more in stocks than on cash accounts. The factors that affect the risk tolerance's calculation may include your age, level of income, and your level of comfort. You have a conservative investment strategy when you are scared of losing money. An aggressive investment strategy enables you to reach for the greatest returns with no worries of the loss effect that may occur.

- **Be aware of your ideal strategy.**

You need to come up with a strategy that will assist you in calculating your returns. Assets with high risks tend to generate greater returns. An asset mix assists you in reducing losses in situations of the poor performance of the asset classes.

- **Diversify your investments.**

Select a wide variety of investments in the market. You should not rely on one asset class. You can achieve this by using either bonds or cash assets of various sizes of companies that have different objectives.

- **Do reviews.**

It's the part where you need to check the performance of your account regularly to ensure you are on the right lane in terms of the time horizon and the formulated goals.

Mutual funds pay for their dividends to the investor who can generate some funds from the investment according to its type of index. Bond indices have a monthly payment of their dividends.

Bond Index Fund

It invests in a pool of funds to monitor the index's performance. It provides investors with the opportunity to purchase its products that can either be a bond mutual fund or an ETF. The products are simple and less expensive for bond investment. Most investors employ bonds to generate income or even to control risks when investing in less volatile securities than stocks. Both products pay dividends that are payments received from companies investing in the bonds. You can purchase or even sell the bond products through a brokerage account where you are required to pay a certain fee.

What is a bond ETF?

It's a type of an ETF that supports investment in bonds or even treasuries. Trading an ETF at any time makes it more liquid as compared to mutual funds. One of the benefits of owning a bond ETF is that you can receive payments on an agreed schedule.

The main downside of this type of product is the great potential risks of the initial investment. It's the type of bond that does not mature. There is no guarantee that it will repay your principal, unlike the mutual funds. Moreover, when the rate of interest increases, the price of the ETF becomes at risk.

Let us now narrow down into the bond mutual fund.

Investing in mutual funds has become the goal of any investor nowadays. What's a bond mutual fund? It's a fund that provides investment on bonds. There exist different types of bond mutual funds that you can employ for your investment.

Municipal bond funds.

These are funds provided by the local governments to provide investment for school and even bridge projects.

Corporate bond funds.

These are bond funds that cover the operating expenses of a corporation. A corporation provides bond funds as a debt. It is the type of bond mutual fund that is not backed by any government institution.

International bond funds.

They provide investment to foreign government institutions' bonds.

Benefits of employing bond mutual funds

- Bond mutual funds are known as active strategies for investment. They provide investors with stable income during recession times in the market, unlike other market securities such as stocks. Stock securities don't perform well during market imperfections.

- It's an efficient method for small investors. An investor can invest small amounts or even systematically make trades on the market. It's the best strategy for small investors.

What is the Difference between the Two Bond Funds?

- Deciding on what type of bond to employ is very crucial. You need to employ the right bond fund that aligns with your objectives. Investors who have active management prefer using bond mutual funds other than the ETF type.

- ETFs are tradable. You can make trades on ETFs at any time in the day, unlike the mutual funds that allow you to make trades once in a day. ETFs also allow you to sell on short and purchase on margin.

- Low cost. ETFs are simpler and cheaper to employ. Its system minimizes all the paperwork and does the recording, therefore, contributing to a lower expense ratio.

Bond Mutual Funds and ETFs Performance

- They have lower expense ratios and tax rates as compared to other investment strategies. They are the best investment strategies to employ for any investor in the market.

- You can generate greater returns from the bond mutual funds and ETFs than the ordinary bond mutual funds.

Stock Index Fund

It comprises of the stock index mutual fund and the ETFs. Stock mutual funds provide investment in individual stocks belonging to public companies in the market. When selecting a stock fund, you need to put the following factors under consideration:

- The style for investment. A stock fund provides investment either on the value or growth. It assists you in not only generating income but also grow in your investment. It is not seen in other funds.
- The size of the company. The funds select the right size of the company to provide investment. A company can either be small, medium, or even largely capitalized.

Take a look below on the different benefits of investing using stock mutual funds.

- It enables diversification. Individuals can invest in more than one stock in the market, contributing to less potential for risks.
- It is simple to invest in the funds. Most of the mutual funds' companies pose reasonable and lower fees for the initial investment with no transactional costs for deposits and withdrawals.

Stock mutual funds have their downsides too that include the following:

- Wide variety of choices. Selecting an individual fund from a pool of choices can be difficult sometimes. In situations where you decide to purchase a fund, you may find a pool of funds to choose from that are on the NYSE list.

- High fees charged on trades. When you make a purchase or any sale of the stock mutual funds, you need to pay for the expenses known as loads that can be unaffordable for most of the small investors.

On the other hand, stock ETFs are assets that track and monitor the performance of an index. They have price adjustments at any time in the day, unlike the mutual funds. You can purchase multiple funds that will limit any risks that may arise in the company's stock. Most investors prefer the ETFs to mutual funds because of their lower expense ratios and operating expenses. It, therefore, becomes suitable for the small investors who will have to incur low charges.

What are the differences between the mutual and the index funds?

The main objective of the index funds is to align with the return gains of the principal (benchmark) index and therefore have the same performance. Conversely, mutual funds have the objectives of defeating the index's returns.

Index funds have passive strategies for investment and are not active in making trading, while mutual funds have active strategies for investment in securities. The management teams, who are active in selecting the right market holdings, pick the best holdings for better performance in the market.

Mutual funds have a higher expense ratio of 0.82% than the index funds (0.09%). As you have seen earlier, mutual funds are unfavorable for small investors because of their high charges. (Yochim, 2019)

Chapter 8

Fundamentals of Investments

As an investor, it is crucial to familiarize yourself with vital elements of investments so that you may be adequately informed on aspects of investment. The following is a highlight of these investment matters.

Investment Goals/Reasons

When investing, you must have goals. The following is a brief description of some of the goals.

- Grow your money: investing in an index fund will offer you returns over a long period of time

- A way of saving for retirement: It is vital to consider saving for your retirement in the form of investment. You may consider investing in stocks, mutual funds, businesses, or real estates

- Earn a lot of returns: If you want your investment to give you the best returns, then research and get an investment vehicle with the best rate. Therefore, if you have a substantial amount of money at your disposal, think of investing it

- Attain your financial goals: By investing in an index fund, your money would be earning a higher rate of return than in a saving account. Therefore, the return you will get will help you meet your financial plans – buying a car, taking children to school, and buying a home.

Who Should Invest in an Index Fund?

This investment is ideal for an investor who wants to create wealth within an extended period of time but has no confidence in fund managers. With an index fund, the notion of management bias is removed, and investors feel free to invest their money with it.

Tracking Errors

Bear in mind that index funds work by mirroring the index they are tracking. However, the returns of the index funds always seem to be much lower than the index they are tracking. This difference is referred to as tracking errors.

The magnitude of tracking errors depends on several factors – corporate actions, changes in the composition of an index, inflows or outflows in the fund, and liquidity levels of the fund.

Chapter 9

Investment Principles

Before you invest in an index fund, it is essential to familiarize yourself with investment principles. The following is a brief highlight of these elements.

Risks and returns

Before you invest in anything, bear in mind the trade-off between risks and returns. Consider selecting a portfolio based on the levels of risks you are comfortable with. Please note that various types of investments have unique risks; for instance, stocks are riskier than bonds. It is vital to note that the higher the risk, the greater the returns in investments.

Diversification

This is one of the best principles you need to take into consideration because it will help you spread your investment risks and enhance your chances of getting high returns.

Long-term investment

Avoid short-term investments that are based on market timings.

Rebalance your investment

This is ensuring that your investment portfolio remains aligned to your desired allocation. Note that as time goes by, the value of assets in your portfolio might fluctuate due to changes in market conditions.

When the portfolio drifts from its initial weightings, its risk varies too. If the deviation is as a result of an increase in the value of an asset, then it can be concluded that asset is a highly risky one. If the trend continues that way, then your portfolio will have the biggest proportion of risky investments. Therefore, the best remedy for this scenario is to do rebalancing. This implies that you will have to either buy or sell some assets to restore the portfolio allocation to meet your set objectives.

Effective management of costs

If you want to avoid incurring huge transaction costs, then consider a passive investment. This mode of investment has an objective of not outperforming the benchmark index but to mirror. Therefore, you are likely to incur low charges when you inject your money in an index fund or ETF.

Beware of risk

As you invest, take into consideration that your portfolio is exposed to market risks. The value of your investment may rise or fall within a particular time.

Different Structures of Index Funds

As an investor, it is essential to know the various structures of index funds. The following is a brief description of them.

- Exchange-Traded Funds (ETFs): An investment fund whose shares are traded on the stock exchange. It is crucial to note that these products are transacted throughout the day and through brokers. For more details about ETFs, please refer to chapter four of this book.

- Open-Ended Investment Companies (OEICs): This is a pooled fund akin to a unit trust. However, it is created under company law rather than trust law. Therefore, OEICs issues shares instead of units. It is vital to note that these shares are not traded on the stock exchange.

- Unit Trusts: This is a mutual fund structure that provides a framework for funds to hold assets and provide income to individual investors instead of reinvesting it. They are traded daily. As modes of investments, unit trusts are open-ended, meaning that the manager can produce or terminate the units based on the demand.

- Investment Trusts: This is a fund with a limited number of shares. It is primarily established to invest in other companies. Note that investment trusts trade like shares on the stock market throughout the day.

- Mutual Funds: These are trusts that collect funds from various investors with common financial goals and devote the funds in varied asset groups depending on the investment objectives. Mutual funds can be defined as financial intermediaries that are set up to professionally manage money pooled from different investors (Robert Pozen, Theresa Hamacher, 2015). They can be defined as collections of bonds or stocks.

For more in-depth information about these structures, refer to the next chapters in this book.

Chapter 10

Exchange-Traded Funds (ETFs)

What is an ETF?

An ETF is a form of an index fund designed to replicate the performance of an underlying index. It constitutes a group of assets that mirror a particular index. As investment instruments, ETFs are traded at the stock exchanges, and investors can buy or sell them at any time based on the accomplishment of a particular portfolio. As an investor, note that once you buy an ETF, you trade it through your brokerage account just as stocks.

History of ETFs

ETFs came into being in 1989 through S&P 500, and it was first traded on the American Stock Exchange. Later on, the products started trading in the Toronto Stock Exchange (TSE) in 1990. During that time, TSE tracked 100 shares.

In 1993, the first ETF, Standard & Poor's Depository Receipts (SPDRs), was introduced. The primary role of SPDRs was to track the S&P 500 index.

ETFs had been operating as traditional index funds until 2008, when the Securities and Exchange Commission allowed the trading of ETFs via active management.

How do ETFs Operate?

The operation of an ETF follows an indexing principle. This implies that an ETF entails pooled funds that mimic the performance of an underlying index. To be precise, an ETF's primary function is to track the return of its benchmark index. For instance, if the index's return rises by 5%, the ETF's return should also go up by the same amount.

You can buy or sell ETFs at the stock markets through brokerage. Moreover, note that ETFs can be sold or bought at any time through brokers. Therefore, ETFs are open-ended in nature. This implies that they can be created or redeemed at any time; hence, meeting investors' needs. ETFs are transacted just like any other entity on the stock markets.

The Creation of ETFs

ETFs are created by authorized dealers only – financial institutions and institutional investors such as brokers. The creation is done in a combination of units of shares (baskets), e.g., a multiple of 25,000, 50,000, etc. An ETF invests in assets that are proportionate to its benchmark index. It is vital to bear in mind that an ETF is designed to be transacted on the market at a price close to the Net Asset Value (NAV) of its benchmark index.

Redemption of ETFs

The units of ETF shares can be redeemed for a portfolio of assets approaching the index and at a particular amount of cash. It is essential to note that the prices of ETFs are based on the forces of demand and supply in the market.

Trading in ETFs

ETFs are transacted through stock exchanges; therefore, to invest in them, you will have to use brokers or brokerage platforms. Also, it is vital to note that there are other players in the market who assist in creating, redeeming securities, and efficient transactions. Therefore, this doesn't involve the traditional fund manager; hence, annual expense ratios are minimized.

You can sell an ETF either at a discount or a premium from the price of its benchmark portfolio's NAV or fair value. Suppose that the ETFs you have invested in is trading at a premium. The prudent action you can take is to sell them and buy cheaper underlying assets of its creation units. Also, if ETFs are offered at a discount to the underlying unit's value, you can buy them and sell the expensive ones. By trading this way, you can fully exploit the arbitrage opportunities in the markets.

ETFs are traded on two types of markets – primary and secondary markets. The following is a brief highlight of these markets.

- The Primary Market: This market entails three players – market maker, fund manager, and authorized participant (AP).

- The fund manager: issues and manages ETFs.

- Authorized participant: These are institutions mandated to trade at the stock exchange. They have the authority to create and redeem shares hence providing liquidity to investors. Note that it is only AP that can create and redeem shares with the issuer. AP creates EFT in multiples of units (in most cases, 100, 000 stocks). The AP then delivers the securities or cash equivalent to the issuer. The created stocks can be disposed of at the secondary market (stock exchange).

- Market Makers: They offer liquidity for the purchase and sell orders in the secondary market for the EFT. They bid and offer prices for the EFTs. Note that when they do so, the difference between the bid and offer price is referred to as bid-offer spread. They provide on-screen transaction quotes at which they intend to trade. These real-time quotes are vital to you because you can make an informed choice based on them.

Index ETFs can be classified into two – physical and synthetic ETFs. The physical index ETF holds all or a sample of the composition of an index. However, synthetic ETFs use derivatives.

- The Secondary Market: It encompasses buyers and sellers of ETFs. Other parties include the stock market, investors, brokers, and advisers. In case you want to trade in ETFs for the first time, you need professional guidance from financial experts. It is vital to consult, especially when you are not sure of investment matters. Other players in the secondary entail settlement or clearing institutions.

Pricing of ETFs

ETFs are sold at the secondary market at prices determined by several factors – the share price in the underlying index, currency exchange rate, and investor's demands. You can keep tack on the ETF share prices through the issuer's website. You can also access information concerning ETF shares from your stockbroker.

Benefits of ETFs

The following are some of the essential benefits you will get by investing in ETFs

Tax efficiency

ETFs generate little capital gains; hence, their tax expenses are minimal. Since ETFs are not actively managed, securities are only sold to reflect variations in the underlying portfolio. Under ETFs, when there are changes in the constitution of an index, portfolio changes have to be made to conform to those variations without taxing the investor since there is no capital gain or loss is experienced. On the other hand, mutual funds tax investors on capital gain if the stocks they hold exit an index. This is because the fund has to sell such shares upon exiting the index.

Lower annual expense ratios

Since ETFs operate under passive management, their annual expense ratios are lower than that of mutual funds. On average, the expense ratios of most ETFs are less than 20 basis points whereas index mutual funds have average expense ratios of at least 300 basis points (Mazumder, 2014). Therefore, it is crucial to note that due to lower costs, investing in ETFs will provide you with better annual returns.

Trading efficiency

ETFs can be bought and sold on the stock markets at any time, just like ordinary stocks.

No minimum amount when investing with ETFs since you can buy even single stocks.

Despite the immense benefits derived from ETFs, trading on these products is done via brokers. Therefore, as an investor, be psychologically prepared to incur brokerage fees when transacting in them.

Top Five Reasons Why You Need to Invest in ETFs

The following is a highlight of reasons why you need to invest in ETFs

An excellent method of diversifying your portfolio

An ETF fund can hold hundreds of stocks and bonds; hence, helping to spread the risks. By investing in all or part of the securities, index ETFs provide a highly diversified portfolio.

Effective management

Once you buy ETFs, the administration of your investments is left in jurisdiction of competent experts. As an investor, you will be given daily updates regarding the performance of the investment you hold.

ETFs are Liquid

Just like stocks, you can easily buy and sell ETFs through the stock exchanges.

Lower expenses

ETFs, like mutual funds, track an index, and they are characterized by lower expense ratios.

Transparency

When ETFs are issued, they are backed by assets of the same value; therefore, the security of your investments is guaranteed. Also, note that when ETFs are issued, a fact sheet is provided showing the amount of exposure and how the net asset value is computed. Furthermore, the publication of tracking performance is done regularly.

Important Factors You Need to Consider Before Investing in ETFs

Before investing in ETFs, it is vital to consider the following crucial factors.

Whether you wish to invest in a lump sum, or through frequent contributions

Bear in mind that whenever you are transacting in EFTs, you will have to incur costs – brokerage fees and bid-offer spreads.

Therefore, buying an EFT via a lump sum is more economical than purchasing it through ongoing small contributions.

If you want to invest in an index fund through continuous contributions, then it is advisable to consider the traditional mutual funds where expenses depend on a small percentage of what is contributed as opposed to a constant amount per trade.

Transaction Costs

Trading in ETFs is conducted through brokers. Therefore, be prepared to pay a brokerage fee either as a percentage or at a flat rate. It is vital to analyze these fees in relation to the amount you want to invest in. If you think that the amount you want to invest is very large, then ETF is the better option. The following is a highlight of various types of costs

Administration fees

These are referred to as Ongoing Charges Figure (OCF). These encompass fees incurred in management, registration, legal, and regulatory expenses in running the fund. OCF costs are paid annually to the fund.

Brokerage charges

Beware that you will incur brokerage fees when transacting on the stock exchange, and the amount of cost will depend on the broker or the broker platform.

Trading spreads

A spread is the difference between the bids and asks price. It is the gap between buying and selling.

Investment Time

Unlike mutual funds, ETFs have cheaper expense ratios; hence, they are ideal for long-term investment.

Strategies of Trade

Investing in ETFs comes with flexibility in trading, and you can apply the best strategies to achieve excellent results. When choosing the appropriate approach, avoid strategies involving regular transactions with ETFs to minimize brokerage fees. For instance, if you are a market timer, you would always place orders to stop any possible loss on your portfolio. This may cost you a lot in terms of fees.

Diversification

If you want to create a well-diversified portfolio, then ETFs it the best option for you. An ETF holds thousands of stocks in a specific class of assets. Spreading of risks is vital to safeguard your investments from losses. In instances where there is portfolio imbalance, ETFs can be used to correct them.

Distributions

Once you invest, you are entitled to receive income at the end of particular periods –at every quarter. The gain received will be based on the portfolio, and it may be in the form of dividends or interest.

However, the amount of money you will get depends on the magnitude of your portfolio and assets allocation.

Chapter 11

Open Ended Investment Companies (OEICs)

What are OEICs?

Open-Ended Investment Companies are the preferred method of stock investment today. In this form of investment, an expert fund manager puts together money from different shareholders and invests it. This method offers you an opportunity to spread your money across various ventures, bonds, and equities. It is an excellent form of investment in instances where you may be lacking the time or adequate knowledge in finance.

How Do OEICs Work?

OEICs work in a very simplified manner;

- You first buy shares in an OEIC.

- The manager of the fund then puts your money together with that of other shareholders and invests it.

- The fund invests in different investments, such as securities and other assets.

- You, as an investor, own some part of the OEIC. Meaning when the worth underlying securities in the fund rises, so does your stock value. Similarly, when the worth of the underlying securities in the fund falls, so does your share value.

- The size of the fund increases and decreases as investors buy and sell.

Structure of an OEIC

Mutual funds can either be open-ended or closed-ended. Both structures are managed professionally by expert fund managers. Also, both of them aim to achieve diversification in multiple asset investments from cash put in by a pool of investors. The operating costs and investment costs are lower since the funds are more and come from many investors as opposed to what it would cost a single investor.

These two forms of mutual funds also differ in certain aspects. With open-ended mutual funds, their shares sell on-demand at their net asset value (NAV). The worth of the underlying securities determines the NAV. The calculation of the price takes place when the day is coming to an end. You perform transactions, such as buying shares directly through the fund. It is flexible in that it allows investors to join and leave at any given time. You can invest smaller amounts of money in an open-ended investment.

Closed-ended investments, however, have a specific number of shares. Trading takes place by exchanging these shares among investors. Potential shareholders cannot join, nor can existing ones exit until the period of the scheme concludes. Unlike open-ended funds, closed-ended funds do not trade at their NAVs. The basis of their share prices is on the demand and supply of their funds. Also, they can sell at their premiums and discounts. The funds are also sold all day long like regular stock at the prevalent cost at any moment of the day. It operates in a real-time manner. Unlike open-ended funding, closed-ended funding only allows lump sum investment, which is riskier, especially if the market turns out to be unfavorable. Open-ended funds tend to be more popular than closed-end funds since they are highly liquid.

OEICs have an open structure. An OEIC makes new shares in case there is demand from potential shareholders. The fund can also eliminate shares of investors who wish to leave the fund at any given time. In OEICs, the NAV from the underlying worth of securities determines the price for use on a specific day. The pricing in OEICs is once per day.

The Benefits of Open-Ended Funds

As an investor, there are numerous advantages to pursuing open-ended funds. Your money is put in with other investor's money making it possible to invest a small sum of money. It makes it cost-effective for you as an investor. The pressure on how to go about decreases since the expert fund manager makes the underlying investment decisions instead.

The fund managers are investing a spread on investments, which in turn gives you the investor a more balanced portfolio of securities or other assets at a reasonable cost. Also, a significant range of investments reduces your risk as an individual investor.

Pricing of an OEIC

With OEIC, you purchase shares rather than units. It makes understanding of its pricing much more manageable since it's on a single pricing basis. By taking the midpoint between the full offer cost and the cancellation, you will get the mid-market price. You will pay this price plus a small initial fee if you want to buy shares in a fund.

Where Can you Buy/Sell OEICs Products?

There are various ways in which you can purchase or sell an OEIC;

- You can buy or sell through an online fund platform.
- You can buy or sell through an online share dealing service.
- You can purchase or sell via an independent financial planner.
- You can go to a fund management company and purchase directly.
- You can also purchase via an agent who has ties to a fund manager.

What is the Difference between OEIC and Unit Trusts?

There are two types of mutual funds; the Unit trusts (or UTs) and the OEICs. Unit funds are mutual fund forms that permit funds to have assets and provide profits that go to individual shareholders. These two funds have some similarities to them. For instance, both are open-ended and have a fund manager who trades for the investors of a fund. The difference between the two is in the pricing. Unlike OEICs, whose pricing is once per day, Unit Trusts consist of two rates. The first is the bid price, which is the cost per unit for when you sell shares back to the fund. The second is the cost you pay to purchase a percentage of the fund, the offer price. Also, the OEICs tend to have a more straightforward structure than the UTs, which in turn enables them to have lower fees. Due to this reason, that is why most investors tend to lean more to OEICs than to Unit trusts.

Charges and Costs

There are several charges and expenses you need to be keen on when investing in an index fund. These costs are what cover the running fees for the fund. The charges are usually taken directly from the fund itself. The fund, therefore, needs to ensure that its performance will guarantee a profit even after accounting for these charges. Below are some different fees you may be required to pay in OEIC;

- Initial Charge: it is a small percentage of the cost of buying new shares, like 2.5%. For instance, if you choose to invest

$200 with the first charge being is 2.5%, you get to acquire shares worth $195.

- Offer price: it is the cost to purchase shares in a fund and is only a single price.

- On-going charges figure (OCF): it includes most of the fees used for running the fund. It contains annual management charge, custody fees, registration fees, and distribution costs.

- Annual Management Charge (AMC): it is the fee paid for the services rendered by the fund managers. It tends to be a small percentage of the value of your shares.

- Exit or Redemption charge: OEICs do not charge this. It is the cost of exiting a fund.

Income Distributions/Returns

OEICs are, unfortunately, not tax-advantaged. OEICs are limited only to tax on income received by the fund manager, which means that taxing of any interest and rental income is at a 20% corporate tax. There is no tax to pay on a dividend. To prevent any double taxation of interest, a fund will distribute interest. The viewing of gross interest distribution is as an expense against income of the fund. The corporation tax on gained profits is not payable in the fund.

Depending upon underlying securities within the fund, you may receive income from your investment in the form of interest or dividends. It will determine how your income is taxed. A fund is treated as a non-equity its market value is made up of either 60% cash or fixed securities. The treatment of revenue from the non-equity fund is as interest. Similarly, a fund whose market value is 60% or less in cash or fixed interest is an equity fund. The treatment of equity fund income is as a dividend distribution — interest and dividends in OEICs taxable. Even after re-investing profit and interest, their treatment is as income for the investor. Also, it will subject to the same tax rules as distributable income.

Capital Gains Tax gained when an asset that's improved from its initial value to more is lost, therefore making a profit. Hence, selling your shares will incur a capital gains tax.

Risks Involved in OEICs

Like all other index funds, there are some risks involved with investing in OEICs. They include;

- The possibility of getting back less than your initial investment is ever-present.
- Some funds also tend to invest in higher risk due to the higher returns possibility. It is essential, your research on the type of assets a fund invests in before joining.
- OEICs help you to spend your risk across significant investments without spending a lot of cash.

Diversification of OEICs

Investments are also prone to market-related risks and are likely to fall at some point. It is a considerable risk to put all your eggs I one basket only for all of them to spoil at once. It is for the reason that diversification is highly encouraged. Diversification of your portfolio is one method of reducing your overall risk when it comes to investing. It can also be a way for you to indulge in numerous great possibilities that you may have otherwise not tried at all. A great way to diversify your portfolio is by using a mutual fund investment. Why not it out through OEIC investing. OEIC allows you to try out a great spread of investments at a lower cost. It reduces your investment expenses and decreases the tax payable.

Investment Styles Used in OEICs

There are two forms of investment styles; active and index styles. Active style refers to a scenario where managers deliberately choose specific investments for the fund's portfolio that they believe will perform better than other investments. The active style relies on the assumption that the financial markets are not efficiently perfect, thus the ultimate need for assessing risks and returns. The limitations to this style investing include;

- Results to higher taxes. Active style investing results in higher taxes as the fund manager may trade more often. Hence the funds being frequently and highly taxed.

- Retarded returns. Active style managers hold more cash than the index style managers, which hurts profits. This effect is brought about by the active investors not diversifying on areas to invest, which often leads to inferior returns.

- Higher additional fees. All types of investments do incur charges in their implementation. The actively managed funds include additional fees to pay for the professional teams that govern. Also, used to cover the transactional costs incurred by more frequent trading in the markets.

Index style believes that it is crucial to predict and profit on future stock prices. Investors using index style believe that all information available about a company reflects its current stock price. Instead of trying to guess the market second, index style investors buy the entire market via index funds. OEIC is a form of index fund; hence, they use the index style of investment.

Advantages of index style investment include;

1. Reduction in expenses. This approach usually has operating fees and general costs than actively managed funds.

2. Minimal taxes. Reduction in buying and selling activities tends to diminish investment-related taxes at a great length.

3. Using index funds. Using index style investing allows one to use index funds, which in itself has many advantages, such as the ability to spread your risk to many investments.

4. Exhibit discipline. Unlike the constant changing inactive style investing, using index style investing allows you to maintain your control during market fluctuations.

If you are interested in the form of investing, use a secure way and with great potential. I would suggest trying out index funding trough Open-Ended Investment Companies.

Chapter 12

Unit Trusts

Meaning of a Unit Trust

It's essential to understand what a unit trust is before we delve further into it. It is an unorganized trust fund system that enables funds to handle holdings and give groups directly to sole unit owners rather than investing them back into the finance. It's an accumulated trust fund placed under a trust deed. Its success relies on the experience of the company in charge of it. However, its definitions vary from region to region. What I mean in Asia, a unit trust is just basically known as a mutual fund.

In contrast, in Canada, it's unincorporated finance that allows income flow through to unit owners (Robson, 1986)

How Does a Unit Trust Work?

The cardinal utility of the assets in a single trust depository you define by the number of units multiplied by the unique value per unit. Units trust incurs costs like management fees; transaction costs, so it's essential you subtract them. The manager who is in charge buys the securities on behalf of the unit trust fund;

henceforth, it is divided into identical units, which are traded to investors. Many groups, though, are assiduously controlled with managers making appropriate decisions they think will make a profit in the market, but in the case of conservative funds that will prevail during volatile during harsh periods.

Funds that managers control continuously have a higher cost due to the fact intelligent managers have been employed for the efficient management of the funds and to make the right decisions. The finance manager ensures that the funds are invested according to their purpose. Still, the overseeing of the fund is conducted by a management committee whose primary goal is to alert the fund manager when any contravention occurs with the fund rules.

The fees included in a unit trust apart from the initial costs also include the management, the administration, and the legal charges, which are always grouped to give you a total expense ratio. The managers aim to reduce risks by unfurling investment across different asset classes. Unit trust funds managers make money by buying the unit price when the prices are low and selling them at a later period when the prices are high.

What Are the Investment Styles for a Unit Trust?

There are two common types of investment styles of unit trusts.

- Actively managed style: in actively managed investment style involves using managers to manage your funds' portfolio actively. They depend on analytical research methods to make decisions in investing securities. What to buy and what not to buy. The right time to invest.

- Index investing: it's an investment style that strategies on a broad market index. Managers will use index investing in the formulating performance of a specific unit.

Different Types of Funds Under a Unit Trust

The following is a brief description of the different funds under a unit trust.

- Balanced funds: This type of investment includes a portfolio which comprises of liquid cash, fixed security funds, and equities

- Equity funds: You should consider this type of funds as where its attentiveness of investments is concentrated in equities or securities of known companies.

- Exchange-traded funds: ETFs are an emerging class of stock items known as an outlay fund merchandised on the stock exchange market. Its investment objective is to attain the same return as a specific return as a particular market index.

- Fixed income funds: You should consider these types of investments as an investment that pays a stable rate of return like government bonds.

- Money market funds: These types of funds invest in liquid cash, which is less prone to risks. This type of investment is more stable, and it guarantees stable income returns.

- International equity funds: Funds under this unit trust are invested globally in global markets.

- Real estate investment funds: With this fund, you invest in real estate; this gives you the opportunity to at least invest in properties.

It's necessary to understand all this type of funds associated with unit trusts to have a clear perspective of the funds that you can choose.

Benefits of a Unit Trust

Investing in unit trusts has a lot of benefits you should consider. Its main advantage is the reduction in investment risk due to diversification by managers who distribute the funds evenly to reduce risks. Unit trust investments generally tend to invest in multiple sole securities. Here below are other advantages of investing in unit trusts:

- Easy to convert into liquid cash: unit trusts enable this because units can be easily be traded, and luckily funds can return your investment to money on the same day.

- Variegation: you are investing in a diversified portfolio of investments. The risks are spread out

- Professional managers: The fund managers in charge of your investment have an excellent reputation, and they are usually the best in making the right favorable decisions. They have to be licensed and have accredited certifications.

- Minimal costs: because of pooling money from different investors gives the advantage of bulk buying. Therefore, dealing with charges is reduced.

- Affordable: you can easily buy this unit trust funds because they are collective investments.

Pricing of a Unit Trust

Funds are priced by bid offer pricing or a single pricing method. You can find details of the pricing method used from the prospectus and the product highlight shield. The price of each unit is determined based on the funds' net asset value divided by the number of units standing. The NAV is computed regularly to show changes in the prices of the funding held by the fund.

In the bid and offer pricing method, the subsidy charges are added to the net asset value per unit while the vindication charge is deducted from the NAV. Bid means the price the investors sell their unit trusts. Offer is the price investors willing to buy the unit prices. Spread is the difference between the bid and the offer.

Single unit pricing method the fund provides an individual quote that shows the NAV per unit. Subscription charges are deducted from the funds early invested while the redemption charge deducted from the vindication proceeds.

Costs Associated with Unit Trusts

You are most likely to incur costs while investing in unit trusts. The fees are either paid by you or the fund manager. The charges incurred include the following

- Initial sales charge: This cost is incurred when you pay the subscription fee to the distributor of the fund. Distributors that charge initial fees don't usually charge redemption fees.

- Vindication fee: this is the redemption fee that you pay to the distributor when you trade your fund.

- Switching charges: this you pay to the distributor when you change from one fund to another fund. When you shift, this is charged if you weren't charged the initial sale charge fee.

- Upfront charges: This also you pay to the distributors when you place new money to the distributors

- Management charge: This fee you have to pay it to the managers in charge of overseeing your trust fund.

Returns: Capitals Gains and Dividends Payouts

Capital gain is a return that is gained after the unit sold for a higher unit price than the original price. You, as the investor, don't have a capital gain until the unit sold for a profit.

Dividend payouts are a reward given to you by the company for investing our unit in that company. But these earnings mostly are kept in the company for future investments.

When is the best time to invest in unit trusts?

To be sincere, you can invest in unit trust at any time; however, it's hard for an investor to predict unit trust marketing conditions. The best time to buy is when the unit price is at the lowest price and sell them at a higher price. The fund managers should have a vast knowledge of the workings of the trust fund markets and take into account fluctuations.

Active and Index Investing Styles

There are a lot of factors you should consider before choosing a more favorable investment style. When looking in cost matters, actively managed cost is more expensive to you than index managed funds because of the management costs incurred. In cases of tax efficiency portfolio of actively managed investment is high compared to index investing. The best one you should choose is index investing.

Why you should invest in unit trusts and not in the stock market

Before we delve into reasons why you should invest in unit trust rather than the stock market, we must first understand what a stock market is. A stock market refers to a collection of markets where buyers and sellers met to buy stock.

The reasons you should invest in unit trusts rather than in the stock market include:

- Stock markets are prone to a higher risk: the earnings of a stock market depend on the performance of the company if the company fails to perform; you might end up experiencing losses. When the company is experiencing difficulties, the price of the stock can reduce.

- Stock markets are time-consuming. You need to understand that investing in stock markets is not a smooth pie. You have to perform market research and analysis to find the most profitable stock. It's a complex task and time-consuming.

I am considering those factors. Investing in unit trusts is better and more secure than stock markets. Unit trusts have a higher chance of earning profits.

Are your funds redeemable from the investments?

Yes, you can redeem funds from your unit trust investments. If you wish to redeem your funds, it's on a monthly basis where you can redeem the funds for free, but if it's regularly, you have to be charged a withdrawal fee. There is no limit to redeeming funds from investments.

The Procedures of Redeeming Funds from a Unit of Trust

If you wish to redeem your funds from the unit trust, you have to issue an instruction to the company either by email or the original form you acquired when investing in the unit trusts. The email address will be your authentication signature but, in the case where you don't have an email address, you have to give a signed request where your name will be used as the verification signature to authenticate the redeeming request. A signature is essential to validate the withdrawal.

Time taken for the redeemed funds to reflect in your account after regaining

The standard time it takes for a request to reflect in your bank account is usually four days, but this relies on the investment company in charge of your trust funds. For some companies, it takes only three days for the funds to reflect. This time is usually after the time of the request.

Can you top up your account?

Yes, there is no limit or restriction of you topping up your account. You can do so as frequently as you want.

Modes of Investment in a Unit Trust

You can invest in cash as a lump sum investment. You can also spend your regular savings and even in the EPF investment scheme.

Type of Taxes you are Required to Pay

You are required to pay withholding taxes. Withholding taxes are charged on the interests you earn from your dividends and incomes from the investment. The other type of tax you are not required to pay is the capital gain tax, as they only apply to mutual funds and stock markets.

Monitoring Daily Prices

You can track daily rates by looking for price information in newspaper advertisements or the company's website where they post price changes whenever it occurs.

Switching of Funds

Switching means selling your units to buy another group. You can do this either online or by filling a request form for your company. If you are switching from balanced fund to money market fund, you are usually not charged. But if switching from money market fund to balanced fund, you will be charged an amount similar to the initial fee charged.

Chapter 13

Investment Trust

What is an Investment Trust?

When you think about an investment trust, what should come to mind is a firm that mostly invests in financial securities. Investment trusts are very popular amongst investors who are only able to spend modest amounts of money. Investment trusts are companies that usually take hold of the shares of several companies and trade them in the stock exchange market, thus generating profits for their shareholders. That helps to broaden the scope for the investors because there is a wide variety of assets and shares. They usually have a fixed number of shares that the fund managers can easily trade in the stock market. In the U.S.A, the investment trusts are registered and controlled by the Securities and Exchange Commission. They have to follow the regulations stipulated in the Investment Company Act of 1940.

The shareholder in this context refers to a person who invests in the company by buying shares. The shareholder can take part in activities such as voting in new directors or even making amendments to the investment policy. The investment managers are aware of how the value of the shares keeps fluctuating and therefore invest when they see an excellent opportunity as opposed to waiting for investors to come on board or even depart from the investment trust. The investment trust is also made up of independent board of directors who perform the following duties: they protect the interests and rights of all the shareholders, ensure the dividend payments are made proportionately, ensure the investment managers are doing their work as is stipulated by the company and come up with the gearing policy to be used.

Investment trusts usually invest in assets such as bonds, property, and equities. I want to give a brief definition of the terms, as mentioned earlier, for an easier understanding. Bonds are securities that ensure that the company has a fixed income. It is a loan agreement between the issuer of the bond and the investor. It is because they are not affected by factors such as short-term interest rates. They help companies as well as governments to acquire funds to cater for their operational costs and to fund their projects. (2019) Equity, on the other hand, refers to all the money that would be given back to the shareholders of a particular company after the settlement of the company's debts and liquidation of all the assets.

An investment trust is a pool of investors' money that is used to buy securities, and collectively buy assets to enhance more significant opportunities. In such a fund, each investor retains ownership of his/her shares. Profits are shared rationally as relates to what one has invested in the fund. For instance, if one investor has contributed 3% into the fund while another has contributed 7%, an investor with 7% is expected to gain higher yields than an investor with 5%.

How does an investment trust work?

The investment company usually offers a fixed number of shares by generating the income necessary for ensuring an initial public offering is in public. A list is made on the exchange market to make it easier for investors to buy shares through their brokers. Gearing is a process that enables investment trusts to grab the investment opportunities in the market. In most cases, gearing leads to an increase in the returns of the shareholders, but in some cases, it may lead to losses if the value of the assets declines. Shares are known to trade at a discount when they are bought or sold at a value that is less than the net asset value. On the other hand, if the value of the shares is higher than the net asset value, then the shares are trading at a premium.

Investment trusts work like mutual funds; the only difference being it has invested money of different investors as opposed to one person. What happens is like-minded investors choose to acquire assets using a fund so that more significant opportunities are presented, and risks are minimized. Investors in this find have no right to make independent decisions. By this, I mean that individual choices are not considered on how to handle assets acquired by an investment fund.

A fund manager is responsible for making decisions on what securities to hold when they should be bought and when to be sold. I want you to understand that in an investment fund, any personal decisions you wish to make on investment have been bestowed upon the manager. Investment fund managers are responsible for doing thorough assignments on when to sell securities or buy securities, which will generate income for you as an investor.

Fund managers are paid to ensure they make the best decisions for investment fund investors. Studies have shown that returns from investment funds have an average annual performance of 12-15%. Such numbers are expected to improve shortly because more investors understand the benefits of pooling their money in funds. Therefore, by investing in an investment trust, you are assured of getting the best results after some time.

When should you consider investment trusts?

Key benefits of investment trusts include management by professionals and a diversity of options for investors to consider. You need to understand no one will force you to confine yourself to one type of security. One is free to choose securities that they feel best suit their financial needs. Goals of investing include earning extra money and generating income from projects.

Fund managers are skilled on money matters, thus will know securities bound to fail and those that will thrive in stock markets. Entrusting these managers is beneficial because they will guide you on when to let go of some securities, and when there is a need to acquire new ones.

When you are a small investor, it would be wise to invest in this kind of trust. It provides a wide range of investment opportunities that may range from property to securities.

Where one has very little knowledge about how to make good investment decisions, the investment trusts have fund managers who have experience in making investments. The independent board of directors will also ensure that your interests are secured.

In case you have a busy schedule, but you want to invest. The fund managers are well trained and have experience in the investment field. They know the best time to buy and sell shares.

Key Features of Investment Trusts

What makes investment trusts different from other funds are the key features below:

- Long-term view: Shares are on a fixed basis, which enables fund managers to have a high level of control to choose when to sell securities or buy new ones. Such trusts offer a sense of stability to investors.

- Diversity: As an investor in trusts, you do not rely on the success of one company, but on a variety of other businesses should some fail to materialize. Investment trusts ensure that such a risk does not affect investors' capital.

- Best interests of investors: You have the right to vote when you invest in a trust. Choices you make as to who directors go a long way because you get to choose the best people to take care of your investments.

- Low costs: Since charges are made annually, they are low on an investor's budget because they are drawn from a trust's account without tampering with an investor's account.

- Borrowing power: Trusts can offer loans to entities with a likelihood of getting high returns, which can increase an investor's assets.

- Closed-ended structure: There is a fixed number of shares, showing that there has to be a buyer and a seller for a share. The size of the investment trust is not affected by outflows and inflows.

- Gearing: It refers to the ability to borrow to make use of the investment opportunities in the market. It helps to increase profits when the value of the share is high.

- The shareholder's rights are protected: The independent board of directors keeps the investment managers on their toes, ensuring that they are performing their duties according to the standards put in place.

- Wide range of investment opportunities: It is because of the large number of assets and securities that are in the market.

Are Investment Trusts closed-ended or open open-ended? What is the difference?

Investment trusts are Closed-ended. An investment manager is in charge of all the activities that take place. The investment company usually offers a fixed number of shares by generating the income necessary for ensuring an initial public offering is in public. A list is made on the exchange market to make it easier for investors to buy shares through their brokers. An investment trust lies in this category.

Investment trusts are closed-ended, meaning they do not have money coming in and out without predictability from fund managers or investors. What do I mean? An investor cannot withdraw money from the trust whenever he/she feels like or deposit more into the trust.

One can buy or sell closed-ended funds at any given time as long as the market is accessible. The market demand for shares greatly affects its value. The value of the shares is, therefore, either at a discount or at a premium.

Open-ended are funds that have an unlimited number of shares. The investors can redeem their shares at any time that they feel is right for them. The sale of shares is made directly from the sponsors to the investors. The investors are free to leave when they feel it is high time to do so.

Payment of taxes is on the capital gains or income generated from the funds. The tax burden is on the investors and not the company.

Open-ended trusts are those that allow investors to buy shares directly from a fund as opposed to closed-ended, which are made available by a company through an initial public offering (IPO). Being closed-ended ensures fund managers have requisites of the best securities to trade in to ensure investors realize a guaranteed profit.

The Unpopularity of Investment Trusts

Investment trusts are unpopular because they are designed to suit small investors. Because they give managers the discretion to call shots on opportunities presented, some opportunities may attract significant losses, which makes investors avoid them as they surrender their power to the managers. Fund managers could be making wrong financial decisions which the investors cannot overrule because managers have the discretion to act alone on behalf of all investors of a specific fund.

A lot of people have very little information about investment trusts. It leads people to believe that coming up with investment trusts takes up a lot of time and has a lot of complications when, in the real sense, the whole affair is pretty smooth. They create enormous investment opportunities that have financial limitations through the large number of assets they can pool. Another reason for their unpopularity is because they use a closed-ended approach. This implies that the creation and trading in their stocks are limited.

Differences between an investment trust and a unit trust

All can be categorized as one because they have one thing in common, which is the ability to invest in a pool of assets. It helps them to reduce the level of risk and widen the range of investment opportunities. However, they all differ in one way or another.

Investment trust.

An investment trust has a large pool of assets, such as shares. Management consists of the independent board of directors and the fund managers. The fund managers are in charge of the day-to-day operations of the company, while the independent board of directors ensures there is consideration of the rights of the shareholders.

It has a close-ended structure and therefore has a limited number of shares. The structure is not affected by inflows and outflows, but instead, it is affected by the demand of the shares in the market.

Gearing takes place in investment trusts to enable them to make the most of the investment opportunities available in the market. It increases the chances of acquiring huge profits, especially if the price of the shares is high.

The creation of reserves occurs by setting aside 15% of the underlying assets each year. When the investment trust is in a crisis, it can use the reserve to pay the shareholders their dividends.

Pricing is done using premiums and discounts. Premiums show that the price of the shares is higher than that of the value of the total assets of the company. Discounts, on the other hand, show that the value of shares is lower than that of the total assets.

Unit trust.

The size of a unit trust is affected by the inflows and outflows. Their size increases when there is a huge demand for shares. The size decreases when there are more sellers than buyers within the company.

There is a lot of flexibility because of the large number of assets and securities that the investors can invest. It may include properties, mortgages, and cash equivalents.

Unit trusts have an open-ended structure and, therefore, have an unlimited number of shares. The unit trusts consist of units that have different prices. The number of units generated increases with the number of people joining the unit trust.

Sectors of Investment Trust

Most investors love investment trusts because they cut across different industries, some of which are infrastructure, real estate development, energy, etc. You need to know these different sectors so that once you decide to invest, you can be sure it is a sector that will be beneficial to you. You can get help from a licensed financial advisor regarding the analysis of sector performance so that you may choose the appropriate one for your investment.

Types of Investment Trusts

Are there differences in investment trusts? Yes, I want to explain the different types so that you can make the right decision eventually. It is vital to understand various aspects so that you may make the right choice.

> **Split-capital trusts:** Investment trusts are known to issue only one share. When they issue more than one share, they are known as split-capital trusts. These are not common because they are limited in nature as they often collapse within five to ten years.
>
> **Real estate investment trusts:** These are the most used trusts because of provisions on unlimited life, and issuance of ordinary shares only. REITs, as they are commonly known, protect the interests of the investors by ensuring shares are distributed evenly.

What assets do investment trusts invest in?

Most investments involve the acquisition of assets, which can be converted into cash (liquid assets). Because of diversity in what investment trusts can invest in, these companies have positively grown to invest in illiquid assets such as private equity, property, and infrastructure. You need to make an investment decision that will see assets sold bring in desired results. The fund manager will guide you on the best assets, which will materialize well after a while.

Benefits of an Investment Trust

As opposed to other funds, investment trusts have advantages that make them the best option for investors who wish to make profits out of their initial capital. I want you to understand these benefits are many, but the major ones are:

- Ability to borrow: Unlike other funds, investment trusts can lend money to enhance investment returns.

- Fixed-term: Waiting for the best public offer to sell shares is decisive on the manager's part because benefits are foreseen. The inability to deposit or withdraw money from these trusts enables investors to maintain discipline throughout the life of the fund.

- Professional guidance: Fund managers are not just people picked from a crowd. One thing to carry from this is that these managers are investment experts who will not offer misguided advice on how the trust should work.

- Independence: The board of directors is independent as they are not drawn from investors in the investment trust. Such freedom ensures decisions made are fair and apply in equal measure to all regardless of share capital. This one benefit should encourage you more on why to join an investment trust.

Investment Trusts and Real Assets

Real assets being both tangible and intangible are prone to damages and destruction, which means they could lose monetary value.

Income that arises from these assets could be affected by changes in economic growth, especially inflation rates. Investment trusts rely on revenue, which sets in at a specified time of a financial year, and any mishaps before that could be disregarded.

Most of the individuals employ bonds and stocks when providing investment in real estate, forgetting the goodness of the investment trusts. Did you know that investment trusts can create plenty of returns too in real estate?

Real investment trusts enable you to have a diversified portfolio, therefore, enabling you to protect the value of your investment and shun from losses. You can use ETFs in real investment for low cost and efficient investing.

Investment Trusts and Private Equity

Private equity consists of capital that is not enlisted on public stock exchanges. Most investment trusts relate to institutions that trade on public exchanges so that a large number of people get the offers presented. Before choosing to invest in an investment trust, I want you to understand that some companies are privately owned and do not trade publicly. Such a scenario will limit your options when it is time to making your shares public, and fund managers want to seize opportunities.

Private equity investment trusts are funds that provide investment on unlisted companies to boost their value to eventually offer them for sale or list them on the exchange platform at a greater price. The various types of private equity investment trusts that exist are those that provide investment in the unlisted companies and also on private equity.

How does an investment trust differ from other funds?

Investment trust differs from other funds because of its unique feature of closed-end. Such a feature is essential because an investor will not interfere with invested money, and will receive financial assistance from fund managers when it is best to sell securities. Other funds have investors depositing cash in the fund, and can make misinformed decisions about share trading.

Moreover, the following are other differences between investment trusts and other funds.

- Investment trusts have extra benefits to its investors as compared to funds. You can borrow loans for investment that lead to your investment growth.

- Investment trusts have a fund board of directors who have the responsibility of assigning the best investment to investors according to their interests. It is not suitable in other funds,

- You gain more returns from investment trusts than on other funds. You pay fewer capital gains taxes on returns that are cheaper as compared to other funds.

- You pay for a lower initial amount of investment in trusts, unlike other funds in the financial market.

Costs Involved when Buying or Selling an Investment Trust

Buying or selling investment trusts is similar to trading on the stock exchange. You can choose to hire a professional adviser to buy/sell shares on your behalf or can buy/sell them yourself. It is cheaper to buy or sell an investment trust yourself without getting services of a professional. Transaction costs involved in buying and selling must be settled. The fund manager of the investment fund must receive management fees for controlling finances. You must consider any additional costs which could arise between processes involved.

As an investor, it is vital to note that any form of investment attracts a certain level of risk. When investing, you will be uncertain of what gains you will get. With that information, you can choose to go on with the investment, which is considered risk-taking. Investment returns are a good thing, and if you are willing to wait for an extended period, an investment trust will be the best decision you ever made. Be keen on specific assets that fund managers choose to invest the money on because some can be destroyed, leading to losses.

Investment trusts are diverse. You should select the right type that matches the needs of your companies. Investment trusts are better types of investment in real estate than bonds and stocks. They will enable you to accumulate huge returns, and you will grow in your investment.

It is important to first look at the type of investment trust that you want or the intention of having one. This is because some investments are for growth, some for income. Choose the one that best suits you. Think about the time you want to receive profits from your investment so that those that take a very long time do not frustrate you.

If you have experience in the investment sector, you could make a plan to ensure that you invest in only what you believe is best for you. If you have no knowledge, you could consult a fund manager for directions.

Once you invest in one asset, you could reduce your chances of risk by investing in many other assets. Investment trusts have many investment opportunities.

Chapter 14

Mutual Funds

What are Mutual Funds?

Mutual Funds are trusts that collect funds from various investors with common financial goals and devote the funds in varied asset groups depending on the investment objectives. Mutual funds can be defined as financial intermediaries that are set up to professionally manage money pooled from different investors. They can also be defined as collections of bonds or stocks.

When money is pooled together in mutual funds, investors can enjoy better financial services. They can buy bonds and stocks at lesser trading prices as opposed to directly investing in capital markets. All investors usually have some shares, which are a representation of their holdings in the mutual funds. When investors purchase mutual funds, they invest their money in multiple companies simultaneously. They spread their investment risks over a variety of companies, thus lessening the risk for loss.

How do the mutual funds work? Investors in mutual funds schemes usually receive some units that are dependent on the quantum of the money they have invested. The units represent the investors' proportional ownership of the assets in a particular scheme, and their liabilities in case losses are incurred. All these are limited by the number of funds that the investors have invested in the scheme.

The most significant source of strength for the mutual funds is pooling together of the resources. When the amounts needed for investment on mutual funds are relatively low, the more the benefits that small scale retail entrepreneurs can take advantage of. The advantages include professionalism in the management of money as well as enhanced access to multiple markets that they could not have been accessed. Fund managers are expert investors who invest in the pooled money in place of the investors. The fund managers work on making investment decisions about choosing securities and how much investment should be made on them.

A set of rules and regulations governs the decisions that are made by the fund managers. The rules are set following the investment objectives and patterns of the mutual funds' schemes. The investment patterns and goals also act as guidelines to investors when choosing the appropriate funds for their investment purposes.

Multiple schemes are offered by mutual funds depending on the state. They all aim to cater to a variety of investors to fit their various financial objectives. For instance, some mutual funds schemes offer capital protection for risk as opposed to investors. In contrast, others provide capital appreciation through investments on small and mid-segments of the equity markets to favor the more aggressive investors.

Investment practices are diversified in a way that they enable classification and sub-classification of the mutual fund schemes. The broader classification of the schemes can effectively be done at the levels of the assets class. Therefore, you have Liquid, Bond, Equity, Balanced, and Gilt Funds. These funds have an additional sub-classification of small-cap, mid-cap, and index funds.

Features of Mutual Funds

Considering how mutual funds are becoming a popular way of investment, you may also opt to try it out. But before you go into it, you need to understand some of the most critical features of mutual funds. Understanding these features will help you to know what you are about to get yourself into and what benefits you should expect. They will also help you to choose the best scheme to invest your money on.

An Expert Fund Manager Takes Care of Your Money

We all know that investment is not one of the most straightforward tasks we can engage in. In several instances, you may face challenges in the financial sector, thus experiencing multiple downfalls. For this reason, you must get yourself some expert guidance as you enter the scheme. Mutual funds offer expert services. In the mutual fund schemes, there are professional fund managers who have the responsibility of taking care of your funds together with other investments. The fund managers have the knowledge and skills on proper fund management and minimization of risks. In the mutual fund scheme, you will find other investors having similar goals to you. Therefore the fund managers will be tasked with managing all the particular investments made in the scheme.

Lump-Sum and SIP Investment

How flexible are mutual fund schemes? Mutual fund schemes are flexible to the extent that they allow you to invest in ways that fit your specifications. They do not have restrictions on amounts or the frequency of your investment. Irregular investments are referred to as lump-sum investments.

However, an option on regular investment is provided. Mutual fund schemes facilitate regular investments. Making regular investments means that you are investing a fixed amount and at fixed intervals. It is referred to as the Systematic Investment Plan. In this particular investment, you are required to make a decision on the total amount to be invested and intervals for the regular investment weekly, fortnightly, monthly, or quarterly.

Returns are not Fixed

The investments in mutual fund schemes are made in the form of shares and bonds. It means that the investment is happening through the shares markets and the bond market. The price of stocks and bonds regularly changes as in any other market. Due to the periodically changing prices, you cannot predict the earnings you are going to make from an investment.

Mutual funds schemes purchase and sell equities and bonds from markets. Therefore, the profits that are made from buying and selling primarily depend on price fluctuations. It is important to note that the amount of profit you can make from mutual fund schemes cannot be fixed. It is dependent on the volatility nature of the market.

Equity Mutual Fund Can Make Loss

Equity is a term given for shares. Therefore, the mutual funds that focus on shares can be referred to as equity mutual funds. We all know that shares' prices go on a roller coaster ride. They may offer you incredible returns in the long term, but you will have gone through a challenging period. Extreme downturns in the markets can occur anytime and without warning, thus making you lose some of your money.

What is the best thing to do? To minimize the risk of suffering such losses, you must identify the best time to withdraw your money from a mutual fund scheme. Do not remove your money during a market downturn, as you may have to bear huge losses.

Debt Mutual Funds are Safer

The returns that you get from mutual fund schemes vary depending on the debt or share market. We all know that these markets are likely to fluctuate depending on the timing. However, you should note that not all markets show some wild fluctuations. There is, for instance, little volatility in the bond markets because the prices of bonds do not drastically change. The returns from the scheme can, therefore, be stable.

What is the best thing about debt mutual fund? Debt mutual fund schemes invest in bond markets and give returns that are almost fixed. It is relatively volatile, but your chances of bearing losses are very minimal. This feature makes the Debt mutual fund schemes much safer than the Equity Mutual Funds.

Many Ways of Investment

Where should you consider putting your money? Mutual Fund Offices are limited, and you may not easily find one in your locality. You, however, have multiple ways through which you can make investments in mutual funds. Below are the forms you can use to make that investment:

- Mutual Fund Distributors- They can easily be found within your vicinity. The mutual fund distributors facilitate the mutual fund sales and get a commission that is agreed upon.

- Banks- Multiple banks are in partnership with some mutual fund scheme companies. You can, therefore, purchase these schemes through particular banks.

- Online Portals- All mutual fund companies have an online portal where they sell their schemes. You can, therefore, purchase schemes from the online portals found on the companies' websites. The portals will provide you with the necessary instructions on how you are going to make your investment.

Charges of Mutual Fund Scheme

There are various costs you are likely to incur when dealing with mutual funds. Bear in mind that some services are offered to you by the fund manager at a cost. The cost of the fund manager, operations, and research team are all paid by the investor. You may not realize you are making the charges because they are deducted from the investments you have made. The deduction is referred to as the Expense Ratio.

How often are the deductions made? Mutual fund schemes make the deductions annually. The amount deducted is used to enhance the smooth running of the company. It helps in ensuring that you are offered the best services.

How do mutual funds and index fund investing relate? Index fund investing is a type of mutual fund investing. It is continuing to gain popularity over the years. Index fund investing is dependent on the belief that it is impossible to try to beat the market consistently.

There is a difference between mutual fund investing and active fund investing. The two differ in that active fund investing involves a management team or manager making decisions on how funds are spent.

Are there any differences between mutual funds and index funds? Many investors have asked this question, and yes, the two differ in several instances. They differ in their investment objectives and management styles. The investment goal of mutual funds is beating investments' yields made from the relative benchmark index. In contrast, index funds focus on matching the investment returns of the benchmark market index. Mutual funds have an active stock picker's management style, whereas index funds have a passive investment mix automated to match the specific holdings.

Benefits of Mutual Funds Investment

As an investor, you need to beware of the benefits that you can get from mutual fund investing. The following is a brief description of these benefits.

- Professional management- Your funds will be managed by some professional fund managers. The professionals will explain to you about your investments and the management of your funds. Mutual fund companies always go for employees who have the necessary experience and knowledge of fund management.

- Economies of scale- Mutual funds have general structures giving them natural benefits. Funds that are pooled from multiple investors ensure that the mutual funds are enjoying economies of scale. Mutual fund investment is much cheaper compared to capital markets' investments, which may involve higher chargers.

- Diversification- Another benefit you get from mutual funds is diversification. Your portfolio is spread across multiple companies, industries, sectors, and instruments. It safeguards your collection from economic downturns in any of the companies, industries, or areas.

- Flexibility- Mutual fund schemes have different features that provide for their versatility. Such flexibility allows you as an investor to build your portfolio appropriately.

- Convenience- One of the best things about mutual fund companies is that they provide convenient routes for investors to invest in their schemes. They allow investors to choose and plan their cash flow needs as per their convenience. Investors also receive the necessary proceeds from their bank accounts.

Asset Allocation in Mutual Funds

Asset allocation is a process through which decisions are made on how investable money can be spread across multiple groups of assets. In this case, you divide your money among multiple categories of assets that do not respond to similar market forces. Asset allocation is dependent on your appetite for taking risks, goals, age, and lifestyle. It may be challenging for you to make predictions on when an asset class can go up, therefore the importance of asset allocation. Once you have your funds spread across multiple assets, the lesser the risks you are going to suffer.

Things to Consider Before Investing in Mutual Funds

It is relatively simple to invest in mutual funds, but there stand a few things you should pay attention to before making your investment.

- One is planning it out. The systematic investment plan is a vital financial decision through which you can invest in mutual funds. It means that you make a plan on the particular amount of funds to be deducted from the bank account and invested in the mutual funds. Plan your expenses to ensure that at the specified period, there is enough money in your account for the mutual fund contribution.

- Second is the timing factor. So when the appropriate time to invest in the mutual fund, can it be when the market is sinking or rising? In this case, it can be both periods. Mutual funds' investments depend on your practice and discipline and not unusually, market fluctuations. So, you should set aside the specific time that you will invest.

- Thirdly is the NAV as of the decisive factor. Investors have used the Net Assets Value as an indicator of mutual fund investments. You must know that funds with lower NAV have higher growth and vice versa.

- Fourth is taking advice- Many are the times you may get reluctant to seek advice on financial issues. You may fail to do this because you do not trust other people or because you want to lead an extremely private life. However, when investing in mutual funds, do some research and seek advice from professional financial advisors. They will help you to formulate a reasonable investment strategy and put it into practice.

- Lastly, the ways to invest- Once you have made a decision on mutual funds investment and planned out the things you now have to put everything into action. You currently have to choose the best way to invest either by purchasing directly from fund houses, financial distributors, or planners or through banks. After all, mutual funds' investments depend on your discipline and the duration of the investment.

Types of Mutual Fund Schemes

Mutual fund schemes are categorized depending on specified investment goals as well as their maturity phases. Basing on their maturity period, they can be categorized into three that are open-ended, close-ended, and interval funds (Fink, Matthew P., 2008).

Open-ended funds are those that are open for redemptions and subscriptions consistently. As an investor, you can purchase and trade the units at NAV prices whose declaration is made daily.

Close-ended monies have set maturity periods ranging from a few years to months. It means that these funds are available for redemption and subscription on specified periods. As an investor, you can invest in the mutual funds at the time of the new fund offer, and later the units can be sold or bought on the stocks where they are listed mandatorily.

Interval funds, on the other hand, have the characteristics of both close-ended and open-ended mutual fund schemes. It means that they are available for buying and revitalization on pre-specified duration. It can be annually, once-a-month, or four times a year. These funds are much comparable to close-ended funds though they are different in the following instances:

- Interval funds are not necessarily listed on stock exchanges. They are not named because they possess some in-built redemption windows.

- Interval funds have the capability of making new units issue on set intervals and depending on the prevailing NAV prices.

- Interval funds do not have a defined maturity period.

How else are mutual funds categorized? Mutual funds can also be grouped depending on investment purposes, as highlighted below.

Equity Funds

These are the growth schemes focusing on equity and instruments that are related to equity. The primary aim of the schemes is providing an appreciation of capital from medium to long-term periods. Such mutual funds are for investors who have a higher appetite for risk and have a long-term investment base. Types of equity funds include diversified, sector, thematic, and arbitrage funds.

- Index Funds invest in companies constituting an index and a related proportion. The focus is on replicating a particular market index and providing rates of return over a specified time, thus matching or being approximate to that of the market.

- Balanced Funds are those that focus on allocating the entire assets within its entire range mix of equity and debt instruments. If you go for this investment, you will be offered a choice of distinct mutual funds containing income and growth aims.

Costs Associated with Mutual Funds Investing

There are some costs that you will pay for when investing in mutual funds. Administration costs are the largest. They are charged by the fund managers to promote the smooth running of the mutual fund. The expense ratio for mutual funds is calculated by division of the entire dollar value of asset funds by the total fund fees. Total fund fees are the management and operation expenses charged to you as the mutual fund investor. The expense ratio to expect in many mutual funds is between 0.1% and 2.5%.

What about taxes on mutual funds? As a potential investor, you may question the most effective ways to calculate your taxes on mutual funds. The calculation is primarily dependent on the mode of investment within the mutual fund portfolio. Generally, the distributions you are going to receive from mutual fund schemes should be considered an investment income on your annual taxes. Some factors are put into consideration when coming up with the amount of income tax you are required to pay.

Returns from Mutual Funds Investment

Mutual funds pay interest and dividends as a way to avoid pay taxes charged on investment income. Dividends are used as a representation of a portion of the profits made by a company. In this case, you will receive some funds for every share you hold in a mutual fund scheme. You will also receive some returns in the form of interests that are generated by the scheme's investments. The interests that you receive are dependent on the amount you have invested upon.

What is the minimum investment period in a mutual fund?

There is no specified minimum period when you want to invest in mutual funds. Your investment period will be based on the kind of funds you choose and the term for the investment that suits your specifications.

Therefore, if you want an investment vehicle where your portfolio will be highly diversified, then mutual funds are the best for you. Also, note that with mutual funds, you can get both styles of investments – active and index fund investing.

Now that you have gotten the perspective of the different structures that offer index fund investing shift your attention to the role of diversification in investment. You need to know what diversification is and why it is useful in managing your portfolio risk. The next chapter gives insights into this crucial topic.

Chapter 15

The Role of Diversification in Investment

What is Diversification?

Diversification encompasses a collection of various types of securities across different economic sectors and geographical regions. When you buy a mix of securities from different sectors, your investment is protected in case one area fails to perform in accordance with your expectations.

Moreover, it is vital to note that investments can also be pooled within or across assets. For instance, for within asset diversification, if you want to invest in stocks, you can buy different shares of different companies. Across asset diversification entails, for example, buying bonds and shares from different sectors or regions. Traditionally, the returns on bonds and shares are not correlated; hence, they are regarded to be highly diversified.

The main reason why you need to think of diversification is because of the unpredictability of the market. Once you invest, your expected returns may not come to reality because of the uncertainties. Therefore, you should invest in a well-diversified portfolio to get excellent returns.

Under normal circumstances, it is challenging to predict capital markets with certainty because of social or political factors, such as currency devaluation, ethnic conflicts, changes in government administration, and many more.

What Determines the Asset Class in Your Portfolio?

The following is a highlight of the factors you should consider when selecting the asset class in your portfolio.

Purpose of investment

This entails the primary goal of why you are investing. For instance, you may want to buy a house, for education, or to cater for other emergencies. The details regarding your objective are filled in the information form to enable the fund manager to determine the right asset mix for you. It is essential to note that the objective you have will determine the nature of securities to be included in your portfolio.

To understand the client's objective, fund managers use a questionnaire to collect the investor's details. Some of the details that you are asked to provide include your annual income, average annual expense, the reason for investing, when to redeem funds, and your level of knowledge with investment funds.

Risk tolerance

This encompasses the magnitude of variance in an investment return that you are willing to bear. Once you have decided to invest, you must be ready to accommodate large deviations in the value of your portfolio. Before investing, research historical worst-case returns for different assets to know the amount of money you might lose during the bad years. To what extent are you bearing the risks? Tolerance may depend on investment time, future income, and whether you own assets.

Time horizon

This is the duration you are supposed to invest until you get your money. Your investment goals determine how long it may take to redeem your assets.

Time horizon includes short term, e.g., investing for 3 years to clear the loan balance is considered short-term; a ten years investment to cater to college fees is a medium-term, and 20 years investment for retirement is regarded as long term.

The History of Diversification

Why is history important to you? To get an in-depth understanding of diversification, you need to get an overview of its background so that you get informed on how the modern diversification came into being.

Traditionally diversification started as a simple approach that coincided with the development of portfolio theory. Later on, efficient diversification replaced the simple one.

Simple diversification was based on enhancing the number of assets in a portfolio to reduce risks (Williams, 1938). This method was dependent on the law of large numbers. For example, investing in 200 assets was 20 times less risky than investing in 20 securities. In the past, investors constructed portfolios without considering the magnitude of the correlation between returns on different investments.

Under simple diversification, efficiency decreased as the assets in a portfolio increased. Based on a law of large numbers, management cost, which was rejected by Markowitz (1952). It is essential to note that a portfolio of 50 securities from one industry is not diversified as that of the same number of investments from different companies.

According to Markowitz, to reduce the variance, you have to invest. You should avoid investing in securities with high covariance among themselves. You should diversify across different industries; a lower value of correlation coefficient means greater benefits from diversification; recommends investing in low-correlated securities; efficient diversification eliminates unsystematic risks and reduces the investment risks to systematic risks.

About Systematic and Unsystematic Risks

What is systematic risk?

This is a risk that affects market returns. What you need to know is that it cannot be traced to a particular risk of individual investments. Macroeconomic factors such as inflation, wars, recession, and fluctuation of currencies are the primary cause of this risk. Also, bear in mind that an organization has no control over these risks, but can mitigate them. Appropriate asset allocation is one of the best strategies you can employ to cushion yourself against these risks.

Unsystematic risk

It is a specific risk affecting the company or industry and can be attributable to an individual investment. A company can manage these risks, and they include credit risk, product risk, legal risk, business risk, and many more. As an investor, you can overcome these risks through diversification.

National and International Diversification

It is crucial to note that you can diversify your portfolios at national and international levels. The following is a brief highlight of how you will achieve this.

- National diversification: This entails dealing with investments within a specific country. This implies that asset allocation is conducted on securities within the domestic market.
- International diversification: It encompasses investments that belong to foreign market securities instead of the domestic ones. Why do you need an international portfolio? It is essential to have it since it exposes your holding to both developed and emerging markets across the world. International diversification involves investing in foreign

securities and currencies. This approach can have substantial benefits to an investor, such as risk reduction. However, research shows that the positive effects of international diversification reduce with economic integration.

Efficient diversification replaced the simple one because research experts realized that the correlation between assets in a portfolio contributed mattered a lot. According to this approach, the positive effect of diversification can be achieved if all securities in a portfolio are negatively correlated.

According to portfolio theory, a mix of securities yields more returns than a single asset. It is crucial to note that portfolio theory is classified into two – the traditional and the modern ones.

Traditional portfolio theory: It postulates that for the investor to eliminate the risks, they must invest in large numbers of securities.

Modern portfolio theory (MPT): According to the theory, an ideal portfolio can be designed to give you maximum returns if its optimal risk is taken into consideration.

The MPT assumes that investors fear risks, and they opt to venture into risky assets than the riskier ones. However, according to the theory, an investor is ready to take more risk if they believe that they will get a lot of rewards from their investments.

Optimal Number of Securities in a Portfolio

As an investor, it is vital to know the optimal number of securities that will make your investment well diversified. Based on the research findings, a diversified portfolio ought to have between 24 to 30 shares (Alexeev &Tapon, 2013b). Also, it is crucial to note that different capital markets have different optimal sizes of the portfolio.

A study shows that the optimal number of securities in a portfolio is based on market conditions, and this number increases during an economic or financial crisis (Alexeev &Tapon, 2013a). As an investor, you need to beware that during harsh conditions, you are supposed to enhance the diversification of your portfolio. Also, note that optimal diversification is achieved by building a portfolio of uncorrelated securities.

Factors Influencing Your Portfolio Size

Before you decide on the extent of investments, it is essential to familiarize yourself with the following factors.

Time of compound growth: This principle is based on exponential growth. For instance, if you start investing at age 30, you will probably spend $200 per month at 9% to build $ 1 million at age 60. However, if you start investing at age 60, you may have to spend around $1500 per month at 9% to hit $ 1 million at age 60.

The amount of money invested: Your objective of investment will determine the amount of money you spend on buying assets.

The rate of return of a portfolio: The rate of return has an effect on the growth of your portfolio.

Asset allocation: This refers to the division of your portfolio across different asset categories. As an investor, it is vital to note that the volatility of your portfolio is minimized if you mix securities with a low correlation.

Taxation costs: As you invest, the purpose is to minimize the amount of money you pay as taxes. Research well and venture into investment accounts with tax favors or benefits.

Once you have decided on your portfolio size, it is time now to diversify it to protect your investment against uncertainty. Research shows that market conditions keep on changing, and if you are an institutional investor, it is advisable to hold at least 60 stocks in your portfolio (Alexeev &Tapon, 2014).

How to Build a Well Diversified Portfolio

Prudent asset allocation entails mixing different securities with various risks and returns to minimize volatility and enhance returns. Therefore, when doing asset allocation, you must consider the risks, returns, and correlations between securities.

Traditionally, portfolio diversification was done within and across asset class. However, in recent years, diversification is done across economic sectors. For example, you can invest in real estate and agricultural sectors because their responses to economic cycles vary. Also, currently, diversification is done across asset classes, within asset classes, across sectors, and across geography. The following is a brief description of these categories.

- Diversification based on asset class: You can decide the proportion of your investment allocation to each asset class. Classes encompass stocks, bonds, real estate, ETFs, commodities, and cash, and cash equivalent. If you want to invest within an asset class, then choose stocks from different sectors with low return correlation or with various market capitalizations. As for bonds, you may select corporate bonds, municipal bonds, etc.

- Geographical diversification: If you want to reap maximum returns, you have to invest in foreign securities and currencies. This is because these investments are less correlated with the domestic ones. For example, if the US economy is under a crisis, then investing in the UK will protect you against losses you would have incurred if you were to invest in the former's market.

Are you a retail investor with a limited amount of capital? Here is good news for you! Consider investing with mutual funds. These investments are inexpensive and highly recommended to small entrepreneurs.

Assume that you have invested in a highly diversified portfolio. What next? It is vital to learn about portfolio risk management so that you have awareness and knowledge regarding risks. The next chapter gives adequate information on this.

Chapter 16

Portfolio Risk Management

What is Risk Management?

Risk management entails the analysis of potential losses in your investments, such as loan default, and taking appropriate measures based on your investment objectives and risk tolerance. Risk is normally examined based on the historical behaviors of something. Take note that the term risk can also refer to your financial exposure. This is what you are likely to lose in your investment should anything fail to occur as per your expectations.

On investment, it is vital to note the relationship between risk and return. When it comes to spending money on an investment, your risk profile will determine your ability to withstand the risk. Therefore, the more risk you are willing to take, the higher is your return. For example, in the US, treasury bonds are less risky than corporate bonds. Since the latter is characterized by a higher default rate, they offer investors a higher rate of return.

Risk mitigation takes place in different areas of finance. For instance, if you are borrowing a bank loan, the credit manager will verify your details before making a determination on either to approve or reject your application. Also, to manage your investment portfolio, you need to adopt the right diversification to manage the various risks associated with it.

How does portfolio risk management work?

Before we get insights on how risk management is achieved, first, it is essential to understand that an investment risk occurs when the expected income deviates. This deviation can be either positive or negative, and it can be expressed relative to a particular benchmark.

To reap excellent returns, you must exercise risk tolerance by, for instance, accepting short-term risks in terms of volatility.

Measurement of Risk

In most cases, Investors use standard deviation as a metric to measure risk. It is crucial to know that standard deviation is a measure of the dispersion from the central tendency. It is crucial to note that this measure can either be positive or negative.

Therefore, to measure risk, you need to compute the average return and then find its standard deviation over the same period. Next, determine the nature of distribution exhibited by the curve. If the distribution is normal, it means that your expected returns will deviate from the average by one standard deviation for 67% of the time. Also, it implies that they will deviate from the average by two standard deviations for 95% of the time.

The following example will help you understand how the use of standard deviation (bell curve model) works. Suppose that during a fifteen-year period (Feb 1, 2002, to Jan 31, 2017), the average annual return from Swab S&P500 Index was 12.3%. The average return represents what happened for the entire period, but it doesn't show us the returns for specific years. Also, suppose that the average standard deviation for the period was 10%. Please note that this standard deviation is the difference between the average return and real return at most periods under the 15 years.

From the above example, your expected return from Swab S&P500 will be 12.3% plus or minus the deviation of 10% about 67% of the time.

Investment risk can also be measured using other models, such as the capital asset pricing model (CAPM) and the value at risk (VAR) model. The following is a brief description of these models.

Capital Asset Pricing Model: This tool is used to explain the relationship between expected return and systematic risks for securities, such as shares (stocks). It can also be used to price risk assets and to generate returns based on their risks and cost of capital. How does CAPM work? The model uses a formula to compute the expected return of an investment based on its risk.

Under CAPM, as an investor, you expect to get returns based on the risk and time value of your money. The following formula can help you get a better perspective of the model

$$ER_i = R_f + \beta_i (ER_m - R_f)$$

Where:

>ER_i=Expected return
>
>R_f=risk-free rate
>
>$β_i$=beta of the investment
>
>$(ER_m - R_f)$=market risk premium

In the above formula, the compensation to an investor is based on the investment risk and time value of money. The components of this formula can be explained as follows. First, the risk-free rate justifies the time value of money; second, the beta is the magnitude of the risk the investment is adding to the portfolio. For instance, if a security is riskier than the market, it will have a beta, which is more than one. However, if an asset's beta is less than one, it is likely to reduce the risk of a portfolio. Therefore, if you have this information, you can build a portfolio with minimal risk and get maximum returns within a particular time.

Value at risk (VAR): This is a statistical method used to measure the level of risk in a portfolio. This approach is used to find out the proportion of potential losses in a given portfolio.

How is VAR important? This method is useful to both the investor and risk manager. For example, you can use it to measure the extent of risk in your assets and then come up with mechanisms to mitigate them.

Risk Tolerance

Risk can be defined as the extent of variability in the returns that you are willing to bear in your investment. Risk tolerance is a crucial aspect of investing, and, therefore, you must be ready to cope with various uncertainties during the investment period.

I know you are an investor who would want to build a well-diversified portfolio for excellent returns. However, it may pose a challenge to you to know where to start and hoe to go about it. For instance, you may get confused about whether to invest in bonds or stocks; and you might not be in a position to know whether to go for long term or short term securities. Don't worry about these; they are normal scenarios. This book will help you with solutions.

Before you venture into the investment, first, determine your risk tolerance. This will enable you to manage your portfolios based on the extent of the risks you want to cope with.

How to determine your risk tolerance: Your risk tolerance can be determined after you fill a questionnaire. The details you fill the questionnaire with will help the fund manager know which risk category to place you. Based on your income, age, objectives, and investments, you will belong to any the classifications: very aggressive, aggressive, balanced, conservative, and very conservative. For example, if you are approaching your retirement, you might be classified under conservative.

The following is a highlight of how you will manage your risks in case you fall into any of the five categories.

Category One: As Very Aggressive Investor

In case you find yourself in this category, then it means that you will put all your investments in stocks but not in bonds. As an aggressive investor, you are interested in exponential growth of your investment, and you can only get this through equity. This implies that you have to take a lot of risks and let your account have 100% stocks.

If you are a very aggressive investor and want to invest in stocks, then consider index fund investing. Why? This fund is characterized by low costs, high diversification, passive management, and excellent returns.

Category Two: As an Aggressive Investor

As an aggressive investor, you would wish stock to constitute a bigger proportion of your portfolio and the rest to be bonds. Your account should have 70 to 90% stocks and 10 to 30% bonds. Therefore, the best thing you can do here is to spread your risk by investing with a mutual fund. This is the only way you will cushion your assets against loss. For instance, if the components in your portfolio belong to securities in different sectors, you won't be affected a lot if one sector underperforms.

Category Three: As a Balanced Investor

An investor in this category has the following characteristics – working and has about twenty years to retirement. At this stage, you would want to attain a steady growth in your income, but you are worried about the market downturn. Therefore, your allocation in equity should be between 50 to 70%. To achieve excellent returns, you may consider alternative investments like private equity, hedge funds, futures, and derivatives.

As a balanced investor, you expect your investment to grow steadily but at a slower rate than the aggressive ones.

Category Four: As a Conservative Investor

When you fall into this category, it means that you have a few years to retirement, and you would want the little risk. This is the time you will keep your money in a place where there is no loss. Therefore, as a conservative investor, you should 20% of your portfolio should be 20% stocks, and the rest be in cash equivalent.

If you don't want to go through the hassles of managing your portfolio risk, consider investing in an index fund. This is a passive way of managing your portfolio without your direct involvement. With index funds, you are assured of getting excellent annual returns, your portfolio is highly diversified, and you incur minimal costs.

I trust that now you have familiarized yourself with portfolio risk management. It is also vital to get insights into portfolio management. This information is crucial for success in your investment. Therefore, proceed to the next chapter for more details regarding portfolio management.

Chapter 17

Portfolio Management

Meaning of Portfolio Management

Portfolio management is the skill of choosing the appropriate investment policy for you in relation to maximum returns and minimum risks. It is the process through which you can manage your investments in the form of cash, bonds, mutual funds, and shares so that you can earn maximum profits in a specified time frame. Portfolio management is about the determination of threats and opportunities, as well as strengths and weaknesses in the prime of trade-offs faced in the effort to maximize the returns made from a given risk. It involves the creation and maintenance of investment accounts. In a more straightforward language, portfolio management is the science of managing your investments.

Portfolio management is administered by a portfolio manager. This manager has knowledge and understanding of a client's monetary needs and comes up with an appropriate investment plan depending on their income and abilities to take risks. The portfolio manager invests in place of the client. They offer counsel to the client on some of the most profitable investments with maximum returns and minimum risks. Portfolio managers should have an understanding of the client's fiscal needs so that they can offer appropriate solutions to them. All clients have varied needs, and it is; therefore, it is crucial to listen to each client's specifications.

The Role of Portfolio Management

Professional portfolio managers have a goal of achieving the investment objectives their clients have. Portfolio managers are classified depending on the kind of clients they are serving. They can either be institutional or individual portfolio managers. Despite being different, their goal is to satisfy the monetary needs of their clients. Portfolio management works through different investment styles.

The Process of Portfolio Management

For the achievement of a client's economic goals, portfolio managers are required to follow a six-step process to add value.

Determining the Client's Objective

Institutional clients make more substantial investments with longer time horizons as compared to individual clients who typically make smaller investments with shorter time horizons. In this step, portfolio managers converse with their clients to understand their particular desired returns, appetite for, and risk tolerance.

Choosing Optimal Asset Classes

Portfolio managers, in this case, are required to come up with the best asset classes depending on the objectives of the clients. Asset classes can be in the form of private equity, real estate, equities, and bonds.

Conducting Strategic Asset Allocation (SAA)

Asset allocation is the course of setting weights for every asset class at the commencement of the investment period. The weights are set to ensure that the client's portfolio returns trade-off and risks are in line with their specifications. Some regular re-balancing of the portfolio is required because asset weights may vary from the initial allocations. The deviation occurs because of unforeseen returns from different assets.

Conducting Tactical Asset Allocation (TAA) or Insured Asset Allocation (IAA)

The two are various ways used to adjust asset weights within portfolios throughout an investment period. The tactical asset allocation approach involves making changes depending on opportunities in the capital market. Insured asset allocation, on the other hand, involves adjusting asset weights depending on the existing wealth at a particular time. Portfolio managers at the point can use either way but cannot use both simultaneously because they are a reflection of different philosophies in investment.

Portfolio managers, who decide to use TAA work on identifying and utilizing analytical variables relating to potential returns on stocks. They then convert the appraisal of anticipated returns to a bond or stock allocation. IAA portfolio managers focus on offering clients some obstacle protection for particular portfolios. They ensure the portfolio values do not drop below the investment expectations of the clients.

Risk Management

Through weight selection for all asset classes, managers can control the amount of style risk, security selection risk, and tactical asset allocation risk assumed by a portfolio. The selection of security risks comes from the SAA actions of the portfolio manager. Directly holding the market index can help in avoiding the security risk selection by ensuring the manager's returns on asset classes are similar to asset classes' benchmarks. Style risk comes in from the investment style chosen by the manager. TAA risks, on the other hand, can be avoided through the selection of similar systematic risks.

Measuring Performance

The final step in portfolio management involves the measurement of performance through the Capital Asset Pricing (CAPM) model. The performance model is gotten from reverting excess returns on portfolios on surplus market returns. The performance measurement generally involves evaluating the success of the portfolio management process. It is at this point that the portfolio managers will look into whether they have achieved a client's objectives.

The Key Elements of Portfolio Management

What does portfolio management entail? Portfolio management is an effort to balance risks against the performance of a venture to achieve some specified goals. It contains some key elements that help to enhance its success.

- Asset allocation- For portfolio management to be effective, it should have a durable combination of assets. The allocation of assets is dependent on the consideration that the various types of assets do not move together, and some assets are more impulsive than others. Asset allocation focuses on optimizing the returns and risk profile of investors. It does through investment in a collection of assets having a minimal relationship to each other. Investors who have very aggressive profiles can focus their portfolios towards more volatile investments. Those who have conservative profiles can load their portfolio to more stable investments. An indexed portfolio can employ the modern portfolio theory because they help in creating optimized portfolios. Active managers, on the other hand, can use both qualitative and quantitative models.

- Diversification- The only thing you can be confident of while investing is predicting winners and failures in the field. Therefore, the best approach is creating multiple investments that will provide broader exposure in all asset classes. Diversification is the art of spreading rewards and risks in asset classes. Diversification focuses on capturing returns made in every sector within a particular time. It is challenging to make predictions on the sectors or asset classes that are likely to outperform the others, thus the importance of diversification. Adequate diversification is conducted within multiple security classes, geographical regions, and economic sectors.

- Re-balancing- The method is used when returning portfolios to their initial target allocation at yearly intervals. It is crucial to retain an asset mix that adequately reflects the investor's return and risk profile. It helps to eliminate the risks of the market movements exposing the portfolio to minimal return opportunities or broader risks. Re-balancing is essential because it allows investors to apprehend opportunities for growth in sectors that have greater potential. Investors can also maintain their portfolio in alignment with their return and risk profiles. It also allows the clients' investments to make positive market shifts. The investor, in this case, can have a higher risk tolerance capability.

Portfolio Management in Passive Investment

Passive investment is one of the investment strategies that focus on maximizing returns through minimal purchasing and selling. The method of investment focuses on avoiding limited performance and the fees that may result from consistent trading.

The main reason why people opt to invest passively is to build their wealth steadily. It is referred to as a purchase-and- hold strategy, meaning that you buy some securities and own them for the long-term. In this case, your focus as an investor is not on making profits from market-timing and short-term variations. Your fundamental assumption will be that the markets will post some positive returns over some period.

Who manages the portfolio? Passive managers conduct portfolio management in passive investment. These managers assume that there is no possibility of out-thinking the market; therefore, they focus on matching the performance of the market. They attempt to imitate the sector performance through the construction of appropriately diversified portfolios of individual stocks.

Passive investing has some key benefits. One is that it promotes diversification. This means that it helps in spreading risks over multiple sectors. Passive investment promotes transparency, simplicity, tax efficiency, and ultra-low fees.

Portfolio Management in Active Investment

Active investment is a strategy used in investment whereby the investor engages in constant selling and buying activities. The activity involves buying investments and constantly monitoring the activities to grab profitable opportunities. Unlike passive investment, active investment involves higher engagements. Active investors focus on immediate profits.

Who manages then portfolio? The active portfolio managers do portfolio management in active investment. They conduct it by considering other investment factors that their clients can engage in.

The method of investment has several benefits. These are effective risk management, taking advantage of short-term opportunities, and allowing managers to meet the particular goals of their clients. Active portfolio managers can easily adjust a client's portfolio to match current market conditions. The managers are also not required to follow an outlined index; therefore, it enhances flexibility. Active investment also allows for efficient tax management strategies to favor the investor. Active portfolio managers can utilize multiple techniques to hedge their investment bets.

Benefits of Portfolio Management

The following is a brief highlight of the benefits of portfolio management.

- Better decision making- One of the best things about portfolio management is its capability to promote quality investment decisions. It focuses on coming up with appropriate data and making considerations form both bottom-up and top-down strategic perspectives. Portfolio management involves adequate research on markets, thus allowing you to understand what is happening. It also allows you to make predictions.

- Proper risk management- It is vital for your business or company to come up with a portfolio management to minimize risks and ensure maximum profits are made. Portfolio management will help you to take risks that will allow you to reach your entire potential and achieve your set goals. You will eliminate cases of overspending that may result from poor estimations on projects.

- Faster project turn times- Portfolio management allows you to strategically align your business projects and ensure maximum value is added to the venture. It helps to ensure that maximum benefits can be achieved in the minimal time possible.

- Increased project delivery success- Portfolio management helps to eliminate schedule delays, poorly defined requirements, mismanagement of resources, technical limitations, and cost overruns. These factors are minimized to allow for successful execution and delivery of business goals.

- Streamlined data and increased coordination- This is meant to eliminate inconsistencies and project conflicts that may lead to business failure. It allows for transparency through quality decision making as well as advanced business performance.

If you are a potential investor, consider time as your best friend. When you begin your investment early enough, you guarantee yourself of better retirement years. Consider investing in conservative stocks and those that have a potential for consistent growth. Doing enough research will help you to make the best out of your investment plan.

Conclusion

Index funds have become the best model of investment because they are less costly, have high returns, and are highly diversified. In the US, recent research shows that the majority of the people who hold the biggest stake in $17.7 trillion in the US mutual funds net assets are the retail investors. This finding confirms that, indeed, Jack Boggle's ideas that index funds were meant to enable retail investors to compete with institutions and wealthy individuals in investments.

Index funds work exactly like active mutual funds. As investment companies, index funds take investors' deposits and issue them with shares. Next, they use this money to buy shares of stock in the indexed firms or to pay investors who may wish to redeem their shares.

Also, the index fund operates by tracking an index? The fund is automated to detect the shift in values of the securities under a particular index. For instance, in the US, the S&P 500 index consists of 500 companies whose securities are traded on the New York Stock Exchange. Therefore, the fund's responsibility is to buy those securities joining the index and selling those leaving the index.

As you select an index fund, note that they are categorized based on the type of assets, technology, consumer staples, transports, size of the company, and geographical orientation. Therefore, as an investor, ensure that you select an index fund handling the sector you are interested in.

Investing in an index fund for the first time can challenge you if you don't know how to go about it. Before you select the fund, determine the best asset allocation before making any investment. After that, select a suitable company to invest with based on expense ratio and the index you want to track.

Buying an index fund requires that you follow the right steps to avoid making the wrong choice. The recommended procedures to be followed are: find out where to buy the fund, select an index, decide where you will purchase the funds, and find out the investment cost.

There are essential things you need to look into to establish whether you are making the right decision or not. Before investing, evaluate the following: the efficiency of the index fund, the cost of financing, returns on investment, risks associated with an investment, and asset allocation.

As an investor, you need to know that there are various structures that offer index funds investing. These entities include mutual funds, ETFs, OEICs, Unit Trusts, and Investment Trusts. In this book, a lot of information regarding these structures has been given; therefore, you can now make prudent decisions on where to invest. On the same note, if you want to invest in index funds, then consider using ETFs.

References

Belasco, E., Finke, M., &Nanigian, D. (2012). The impact of passive investing on corporate valuations. *Managerial Finance, 38*(11), 1067-1084.

Alexeev, V., &Tapon, F. (2014). How many stocks are enough for diversifying Canadian institutional portfolios?.

Bogle, J. C. (2017). *The Little Book of Common Sense Investing: The Only Way to Guarantee Your Fair Share of Stock Market Returns*. John Wiley & Sons.

Dolvin, S. D. (2015). Warren Buffet Criticizes Money Managers.

ICI. (2019). *Fact Book: A review of trend and activities in the investment industry*. Retrieved from https://www.ici.org/pdf/2019_factbook.pdf

Kostovetsky, L. (2003). Index mutual funds and exchange-traded funds. *The Journal of Portfolio Management, 29*(4), 80-92.

Markowitz, H. M. (1952). Portfolio selection. *The Journal of Finace, 7*(1), 77-91. doi:10.1111/j.1540-6261.1952.tb01525.x

Phoon, K., & Koh, F. (2017). Robo-advisors and wealth management. *The Journal of Alternative Investments, 20*(3), 79-94.

Poterba, J. M., &Shoven, J. B. (2002). Exchange-traded funds: A new investment option for taxable investors. *American Economic Review*, *92*(2), 422-427.

Robson, G. N. (1986). The investment performance of unit trusts and mutual funds in Australia for the period 1969 to 1978. *Accounting & Finance*, *26*(2), 55-79.

Siblisresearch. (2019). | S&P 500 Sector Weightings 1979 - 2019'| Siblis Research. Retrieved December 5, 2019, from http://siblisresearch.com/data/sp-500-sector-weightings/

Williams, J. B. (1938). The theory of investment value (Harvard University Press, Cambridge, MA).

Made in the USA
San Bernardino, CA
10 August 2020